DESIGN IN PAPIER MÂCHÉ

DESIGN IN

By CARLA and JOHN B. KENNY

With Drawings and Photographs by the Authors

Also by
CARLA AND JOHN B. KENNY
The Art of Papier Mâché

Also by
JOHN B. KENNY
The Complete Book of
Pottery Making
Ceramic Sculpture
Ceramic Design

PAPIER MÂCHÉ

CHILTON BOOK COMPANY   Radnor, Pennsylvania

Foreword

WHEN we left our home in New York a few years ago and moved to Mexico, it was more than just a change of address; it was a change in a way of life. For a long time we had been engaged in artistic careers (Carla, in fashion; John, in ceramics), both also in educational fields. Our move meant not only parting from old friends; it meant also forsaking former careers.

Fortunately, our new home environment provided compensations—sunshine, flowers, new friends, new things to do.

We discovered papier mâché and fell in love with it. We explored its possibilities. The more we learned about this versatile material the more our fondness grew. We were delighted by the wide range of things that could be made with it. Its strength amazed us; its low cost appealed to us.

To share our joy with others, we wrote a book—*The Art of Papier Mâché* —and this won us many more new friends. We kept on working and experimenting.

We discovered more, much more. We learned how to make furniture of original design, how to achieve unusual effects with light, how to make things for our garden. Most important, we learned more about the value of papier mâché as a source of inspiration, a help to the artist-craftsman looking for new ideas, trying to create forms unlike any that have been made before.

And so, there was nothing for it but to write another book. We hope that our new offering will please the friends we have made and will add to their number.

Contents

stylized bird form. A dowel for a leg. A washer for an eye. A pelican. Light as an element of sculpture. Armatures. A ballerina. Porcelain-like finish. White porcelain enamel. Draping. Building a bicycle. Making a rider. A "feather" pompom. Plastilene. A wall plaque. Modeling a fish. Covering plastilene with paper and mash. Neptune and mermaid. Adam and Eve. Modeling a dragon in plastilene. Cutting the paper shell to remove plastilene. Resealing. A balloon skirt. Découpage. Using a rasp. Wigs and hats. Pressing a basket-weave pattern. Gift cord and bread paste.

tured figure to hold a glass top. A sketch in plastilene. Enlarging. A cardboard framework. A temporary supporting frame. Modeling a figure with strips of cardboard. Reinforcing. Modeling anatomical details. Spirit level. Sponge painting. Gold lacquer.

x

jointed figure. Modeling parts in plastilene. Papering over plastilene. Cutting the paper shells to remove the plastilene. Resealing. Assembling with rubber bands. Making ears. Milliner's wire. A clown with movable limbs.

Yard birds. A pattern for a rooster. A crest made of coat-hanger wire. A dowel for a leg. Rolling and applying mash. Making eyes. More yard birds. Streamlined shapes. A dancing girl (life size). Metal rod support. Preliminary sketch. Chipboard skeleton. Building a figure of chipboard, newspaper, glue and string. Completing modeling in mash. Birds that balance on fingers and toes. Psyche knot with bread-paste flowers. Making a large sun face. A circle of plywood with wooden strips for rays. Making a dome of chipboard. Rolling and applying mash. Transferring a drawing from newspaper to dome of wet mash. Modeling features. Constructing rays of newspaper and mash. Undercoat of red lacquer. Antique gold paint scumbled.

Papier mâché as an art form. New materials. Simplify. Glue vs. paste. Flour paste recipe. Other adhesives. Priming (sizing). Surface treatments. Spackle. Gold paint. Repairs with papier mâché. Sketch book. Sketching in the third dimension. *Don't burn it—use it!*

Photo Series

Black and White Plates

Patterns and Diagrams

Color Plates

DESIGN IN PAPIER MÂCHÉ

Chapter 1 · Getting Started

WE work with paper, lots and lots of paper, paper of all kinds. Mostly our work is done with newspapers and paper bags from the super market (kraft paper).

We work with cardboard, the corrugated material that cartons are made of. This is stiff, it can be easily cut and folded, but it cannot be modeled into shape. There is another kind of corrugated paper which can be rolled, in fact it comes in rolls—we use that, too.

The type of cardboard that we use more than any other is chipboard (also called newsprint board), a flexible material that is used for making cereal boxes and the packages in which department stores deliver suits. This is ideal for most construction for it can be rolled, twisted, folded into shapes of great variety. With a pair of scissors, a stapler and a piece of chipboard one is prepared to create sculptural forms. When we need larger pieces than we can get from discarded boxes, we buy it in sheets about three by four feet. It is made from reclaimed waste paper and is quite inexpensive. (There is a heavier type of chipboard which is stiff; we do not use this.)

Occasionally we buy a sheet of what is called mounting board or poster board. This is a lightweight, flexible cardboard coated on one side. Usually both sides are white but sometimes one side is tan or gray.

Mailing tubes and the paper cores from rolls of paper toweling are just right for many jobs, so are containers, milk cartons, large ice-cream cartons, and such. Sometimes we use tissue paper, paper napkins and paper towels.

Almost all of the paper we use is material that has been thrown away. Now and then we have to buy some large sheets of corrugated cardboard or a roll of flexible, corrugated paper as well as sheets of chipboard, but the cost is not great.

We use other things besides paper. When we need material for reinforcing, we can usually get some plywood from a discarded packing case or some wooden strips, and we don't hesitate to use empty tin cans, plastic containers, coat-hanger wire, and so forth, whenever they help to make an object stronger or the job of constructing it easier.

We use string to hold our work together as we build, and cord of many different sizes to decorate the surfaces of what we make.

Gummed paper that comes in rolls (package tape) helps us in our construction. So do the various kinds of Scotch tape, especially cellophane tape which is transparent, and masking tape which is opaque and strong.

Of course we use glue: the white, synthetic resin type. We use paste now and then, but not as much as we used to. We like glue better.

Our tools are the simplest, most of them borrowed from the kitchen: scissors, paring knives, a spoon or two, a rolling pin. A stapler is a "must" for us and so is a blender for making mash.

Plastic containers—the kind that cottage cheese comes in—are useful to hold glue as we work, and large plastic bags the laundry delivers our wash in—are good for protecting working surfaces.

We need paints and brushes, and varnishes, and lacquers, but this will be covered in Chapter 3.

It's time to get busy and make something. We'll start by cutting a pattern for a box from a piece of corrugated cardboard. What kind of box shall we make? Just to be different, let's make a box that can be used as a vase to hold flowers.

PHOTO SERIES 1
A Rectangular Vase

water, but the milk carton lining can. Our box is now a vase.

3. Preparing to cover the box with a

1. We have cut out a pattern for a tall, rectangular box without a top. This is about the simplest pattern of all. We are going to make a rectangular vase just the right size to hold that milk carton.

2. The sides of our box have been folded together and the joints have been sealed with package tape. The milk carton with its top cut off fits snugly inside. A box made of cardboard could not hold

2

large sheet of newspaper: White glue, diluted half and half with water, is brushed on the newspaper.

4. The box has been brushed with glue, then laid on the paper. The paper is lifted up and pressed against a side of

the box. A paper towel is rubbed over the paper to make sure that no air pockets or puddles of glue are trapped between the paper and the box.

5. The newspaper is wrapped completely around. Now the box is being sealed on the bottom.

6. *A foot:* A hollow square of cardboard with rounded corners is glued to

the base. This will enable the vase to stand without wobbling. The iron washer in the foreground will be glued to the inside bottom of the vase so that it will not tip over easily.

7. The newspaper is folded over the top rim. The construction is complete.

8. Instead of using colors to decorate this vase, we wrapped and glued a piece

of flexible corrugated paper around it with the corrugations outward. When the construction was dry it was brushed with diluted glue, and finally given two coats of white vinyl paint.

A better way to paper a box is to tear the paper into small pieces and glue them on so that they overlap slightly (it is not so easy to handle a large sheet of wet, sticky newspaper and, in spite of all our care, air pockets have a way of hiding beneath the paper and causing trouble later on).

Notice we said *tear*, not *cut*. A cut edge is hard and stands out sharply in the finished work; a torn edge is softer, less demanding of attention. The interesting surface patterns formed by overlapping rectangles of paper are one of the chief characteristics of certain types of paper craft.

A word about tearing paper: Newspaper has a grain that runs from the top to the bottom of the page in regular-size newspapers; from side to side in tabloids. It is fairly easy to tear a newspaper into even strips along the grain, but making a straight tear across the grain is hard to do unless a ruler is held on the paper.

9. Here, on another box of the same size and shape, the method of pasting overlapping rectangles of paper is demonstrated. Pieces of newspaper torn into rectangles about 1 inch by 1½ inches are glued to the surface of the box, overlapping slightly. The bits of paper have been soaked in water first. Some of the paper pieces have been dipped into a container of water and drawn upward so that they remain on the side of the container. This

allows excess water to roll off and makes it easy to pick up the dampened pieces with the brush.

10. Binding the top edge of the box: Here some of the dampened bits of paper

have been laid on a paper towel. This method also makes it easy to lift the pieces with the brush. With this step, a second box vase has been constructed.

This box will be put aside for awhile. In Chapter 2 we shall cover it with mash and decorate it.

Cardboard vases are so easy to make that they are ideal for trying out colors and ways of ornamenting. Before we begin to explore decorating techniques it might be a good idea to make a few more vases.

PHOTO SERIES 2
Cylindrical Vases

1. We have an empty plastic bottle with the top cut off. What is left will make a good liner for a cylindrical vase.

We have cut a piece of chipboard 9 inches wide (2 inches wider than our

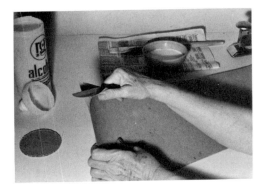

bottle is tall) and 22 inches long—enough to wrap around the bottle twice. A circle whose diameter is the same as that of the bottle (3 inches in this case) has been cut from corrugated cardboard.

Feathering

Chipboard has thickness. If we just wrap it around and glue it, the seam will show as an ugly ridge. To avoid this we peel away some of the chipboard at the end of the strip to reduce its thickness. It will make the seam less prominent. This is called *feathering*.

2. Here we are rolling and gluing the chipboard cylinder. The glue has been diluted half and half with water. A piece

of newspaper is rolled around the bottle first to prevent the chipboard from sticking to it.

3. The cylinder has been rolled and

fastened with a stapler. Here a strip of package tape is glued over the joint.

4. An iron washer is glued to the cardboard base.

5. The base with the weight attached has been inserted in the cylinder and pushed in about ½ inch. The bottle is

5

still inside. Strips of newspaper and glue are used to seal the base in place. Pushing the base into the cylinder, as we have done, provides the vase with a foot.

6. The cylinder is then covered with rectangles of newspaper about 1½ inches by 2½ inches and put aside to dry.

Antiquing

7. After the vase had dried it was given two coats of white vinyl exterior paint. This is a water-base paint that dries hard and waterproof. When that was dry, a coat of white enamel was brushed on.

Here the artist is applying a thin mixture of dark green and yellow ochre acrylic paint to a portion of the surface. This is the first step in *antiquing*.

8. The color is allowed to set for one minute (the brush is put into water immediately—never allow acrylics to dry on a brush). A paper towel is used to rub

the color into the surface. This is *scumbling*.

9. The artist rubs off all the excess color with a clean paper towel. Some color remains, accenting the pattern made by the squares of newspaper and even showing the texture of the underlying chipboard. This vase is shown again (Color Plate 1).

10. A variation of the form we just made using corrugated paper. In order to have a smooth seam, two corrugated

strips are separated from the backing and are cut off. This operation is similar to the feathering in Step 1.

11. The corrugated cylinder needs an inner lining to hold its shape. A layer of newspaper without glue is rolled around the bottle first as a temporary shield. Here more thicknesses of newspaper are rolled round and glued together. These will form the lining.

12. The corrugated paper is glued to the lining. When this step is completed, the vase will be wrapped in several more thicknesses of newspaper *without glue* and held by rubber bands until the construction dries. (The wrapping of news-

paper is put on to keep the rubber bands from marring the surface of the corrugated paper.)

13. Having dried overnight, the portion of the lining which projects beyond the cylinder now is cut off with a paring knife.

When this vase was brushed with diluted glue, then given two coats of white acrylic paint, and a thin coat of coral acrylic was scumbled on. (When color is scumbled on, texture is added to the surface. Since the pigment is put on unevenly, some parts of the object have a deeper tone than others.) This vase is also shown in Color Plate 1.

Before we consider more decorating techniques, we must learn about the most important material of all—*paper mash*.

Chapter 2 · Mash

THE vases in Chapter 1 are paper constructions—not papier mâché. For that we must prepare mash.

We have gotten best results from a mash made from paper pulp with these additions:

Whiting (calcium carbonate). This is a white powder that has many uses. Mixed with water it is whitewash; mixed with linseed oil it becomes putty. When added to mash it acts as a filler, making the finished work denser and more solid. It is sold in paint stores.

Linseed oil is a vehicle. It makes the mash more workable and the finished pieces tougher. It too is sold in paint stores. It can be bought raw or boiled. Either will serve, but the raw is cheaper.

Glue is the binder. We use the white, synthetic resin glue sold under many trade names.

Oil of wintergreen or oil of cloves acts as a preservative and keeps the mash from going sour too quickly.

This recipe makes one quart of mash:

    4 sheets of full-size newspaper (16 pages)
    2 tablespoons of whiting
    4 tablespoons of white glue
    1 tablespoon of linseed oil (raw or boiled)
    2 drops of oil of wintergreen or oil of cloves

Tear the newspaper into small pieces (about 1½ inches), throw them into a container of water to soak for an hour or so.

After the paper has soaked, use a blender to beat it to a pulp. Work with small batches at a time and use plenty of water. Stir in the blender for about five seconds. This produces a good working mash, but if a finer textured mash is required, it should be allowed to blend for a longer period. After blending, the paper pulp is strained to remove most of the excess water.

8

The pulp is put into a bowl, the whiting is *sprinkled* in and stirred into the pulp. (*Don't* use the blender for this step.) Then the glue and the linseed oil are added and the drop of oil of wintergreen or oil of cloves and the whole mixture is stirred—or better, squeezed through the fingers to assure thorough mixing.

White mash: A white mash suitable for work in which a white porcelain-like finish is sought can be made out of white paper napkins and paper towels. A good quality of white toilet paper makes an excellent mash without the need for blending. One roll is enough for two quarts of mash.

Ready-mix mash: Art supply manufacturers have prepared a variety of papier mâché flour which, when mixed with water, is ready to use as papier mâché. For small pieces this ready-mix flour is fine, but for large work it can prove expensive.

Using Mash

When we have made our mash we will have a bowl filled with a grayish mixture, quite soft and very wet. In many ways this mixture resembles clay. It can be modeled into shapes; it can be given a smooth surface by pressing it with a knife or spoon; it can be rolled into layers between sheets of newspaper.

But mash is not entirely like clay. It is so soft that it is difficult to model any form larger than a few inches high. You can take a fistful of mash and squeeze most of the water out of it, but that, while making it firmer, also makes it harder to handle. Instead of responding readily to the pressure of the fingers, it becomes obstinate and tends to form lumps. For these reasons mash is usually applied to the surface of a core made of paper, cardboard, wood or other materials. In spite of its difficulties, some sculptors model directly with mash, treating it the same way as they would treat clay.

The surface of mash can be made quite smooth by "buttering" it with a knife or a spatula. However, the smoothness disappears as the mash dries so that the final surface has a characteristic, rough grain—a texture quite pleasing in many types of work. If we want a smoother surface we have to give the mash another treatment with the spatula when it is almost dry. In this state mash resembles what the potters call the "leather-hard" condition of clay. The material no longer can be modeled, but the surface can be made smooth and this smoothness will remain after the work has dried. When a surface like that of porcelain is desired, the artist must use gesso.

Gesso

Gesso is a material for sealing surfaces and making them smooth. The old masters prepared their canvases and wood panels for painting by sizing them first with a gesso they made from plaster of paris and glue. We have found through experimentation that we get good results from a mixture of whiting, glue, linseed oil and water.

Recipe for Gesso: Sprinkle two tablespoons of whiting into a container of water and allow it to settle. *Don't stir!* After it has stood for a short while, pour off all the excess water. Add one tablespoon of white glue and one teaspoon of linseed oil (raw or boiled) and stir thoroughly. The mixture should have the consistency of thick cream. If it is too thin, sprinkle in more whiting and stir until it is smooth.

Gesso is an excellent treatment for the surface of papier mâché. It seals pores, covers rough spots, and dries with a hard, white surface that is good as a base for paint.

Applying Mash

Mash can be put on a cardboard construction with a spoon, a brush, or just with the bare hands. In any case, the surface that is to receive the mash must be brushed with glue first, and the mash must be pressed firmly in place.

When an object is composed of mostly flat surfaces, mash can be rolled into a layer between sheets of newspaper and then lifted onto the piece this way.

PHOTO SERIES 3
Applying Paper Mash

1. Another rectangular box vase has been made of corrugated cardboard and the top rim has been sealed with bits of newspaper. The box has been brushed with glue. A wad of mash has been put on a sheet of newspaper and is being patted into a pancake shape with a spoon. After this step another sheet of newspaper is laid on top of the pancake of mash and a rolling pin is used to roll the mash into a thin layer of even thickness.

2. After the rolling, the top sheet of newspaper is peeled off revealing the layer of mash underneath.

3. The box is laid on the mash. The newspaper is lifted up so that the mash wraps around the box.

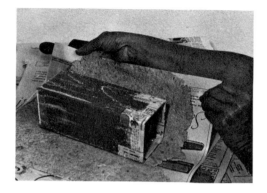

4. A spatula is used to press the mash firmly against the sides of the box. When the entire outer surface and top rim of the box have been covered with mash the construction is finished. (The completed box is shown in picture 2 of Photo Series 4.)

After a layer of mash has been applied, it can be treated in many different ways. More mash can be put on and built up into a form quite different from the underlying core, or small portions of mash may be added and modeled into surface decorations.

Tools of various shapes such as dowel sticks, spoons, and the like can be pressed into mash before it dries to create surface designs. Mash can be pressed into molds to make small objects such as earrings, or to make ornaments to attach to the surfaces of furniture.

Texturing

As we said earlier, when mash dries its surface develops a rough, pitted texture that is characteristic of the material and is just right for most work. Different textures can be achieved by rolling mash on a fabric with a coarse weave, a piece of monk's cloth or burlap sacking, or even a rubber shower mat that is perforated with evenly spaced holes. A fork pressed into damp mash so that it creates various crisscross patterns is worth experimenting with.

Drying Mash

The drying of mash can be hastened by putting it in strong sunlight or in an oven. Take care in using an oven; temperature should not be over 150°F. An object should not be allowed to scorch. Keep the oven door propped open slightly and examine the work at frequent intervals. Remove it from the oven as soon as it feels dry to the touch.

Warping

Paper constructions covered with mash are apt to warp as they dry. In most work a little warping doesn't matter, but we try to eliminate warping entirely when making such things as tabletops. These must be allowed to dry slowly under weights. (More about this in Chapter 11.)

Chapter 3 · Decorating

WHEN an object made of paper is to be colored or decorated, the surface should be primed first. The best way to do this is to brush on one or two layers of diluted glue. When the glue has dried, the piece should be given one or two coats of white vinyl exterior paint.

The way an object is made and the material it is made of often suggest to the craftsman what the finished surface should be. We saw this in Photo Series 2.

Since our work is with paper, it seems proper that we should explore the ways of decorating with paper.

Gift Wrappings

The colorful papers used to wrap gifts need not be thrown away the morning after Christmas; they can be used to color and to decorate some of the pieces we make. Plain-colored tissue paper can be used for coloring flat areas on objects, and the papers with printed patterns can be cut and glued on to make gay surface designs. We shall see this method used in Photo Series 6 and in many of the series that follow.

Découpage

Another method of decorating is to cut out colored pictures from magazines and glue them on. Metal lunch boxes have been ornamented this way to serve as handbags and large cardboard ice-cream cartons have been turned into wastebaskets. Plate 1 is an example of *découpage*. A small styrofoam ice bucket we used on our bar was broken. We glued it together, and to cover the marks of the repair, we painted the ice bucket with white vinyl and then cut pictures from colorful magazine ads and glued them on. The inside and the outside of the ice bucket were then given two coats of marine varnish.

Plate 1. Découpage

Montage

This is another method of cutting out and gluing on. Here the things cut out are usually not pictures, but areas of color and shape that form abstract designs when combined. Sometimes a montage is made of type and typographic ornaments, like the decoration of the elephant (Plate 2).

Another kind of montage can be made by tearing pieces of colored tissue paper and gluing them on the object so that they form decorative patterns. The overlapping of different colors adds another dimension to the design.

Paper that is to be glued on for decoration should be sprayed with a fixative first. After the ornamentation of the object is completed and the glue has thoroughly dried, the work should be given several coats of lacquer or varnish, either brushed or sprayed on.

Cord Decoration

Applied ornaments made of various sizes of cord are well suited to papier mâché.

Plate 2. Montage

PHOTO SERIES 4
Decorating with Cord

1. A pattern is being formed on the side of one of the box vases made in Photo Series 1. Glue is brushed onto the surface of the piece, then the cord is put in place and held by pins (a thimble is necessary here). When a portion of the pattern has been outlined with cord, more glue is brushed over the cord and the portion of the box to which it is attached.

The design could have been drawn on the vase first; here the artist is working freehand. (Note: in this case, the decoration was applied before the object was given its base coat of white paint.)

2. The cord decoration has been completed and allowed to dry; the piece has been given two coats of white vinyl paint.

When the white paint was thoroughly dry, a thin coat of yellow acrylic was brushed on. The yellow was allowed to dry hard, then a thin coat of dark yellow-green was brushed on and wiped with a paper towel. The raised cord trapped color around it so that the design was accented. A bit of hot-pink color was placed in part of the design.

3. The finished decorated vase. Another rectangular vase with a cord decoration of a different type is shown (Color

Plate 1). The surface of this vase was *antiqued* with yellow ochre acrylic, then the cord design was applied and painted gold.

14

Another vase covered with mash was given a coat of green acrylic paint, then a thin coat of aqua acrylic was scumbled over the entire surface. After this had dried, gold lacquer was brushed lightly over the entire vase, then a second heavier coat of gold lacquer was brushed over the upper portion and allowed to dribble downward in places.

This method of decoration enhanced the rough texture of the mash surface making it an integral part of the design.

Coloring

Practically any paint and any method of putting paint on a surface can be used to decorate papier mâché. We have tried everything in the way of pigments that we could lay our hands on (including instant coffee and milk, which we don't recommend any more because bugs have eaten some of the finished product).

Among the things we have used successfully are tempera colors, casein colors, transparent water colors, exterior paints—both water-base and oil, auto lacquers, vinyl paints, acrylics, oil colors, fluorescent paints—both oil and water-base, deck paints, marine varnish, metal lacquers and enamels.

For finishing final surfaces we have used clear lacquers and varnishes of both the brush-on and spray-on types. Where pieces are intended for outdoor use and exposure to the weather, we have used liquid silicone as a sealer before applying any paint.

We have applied color with brushes, sponges, paper towels. We have sprayed color onto surfaces or through stencils. We have used stamping devices—block prints cut from vegetables such as potatoes, carrots, and onions. We have experimented by using dyes in mash (we don't recommend it).

After trying practically everything, we have narrowed our field so that all of our work now is given priming coats of diluted glue (or silicone if intended for outdoors), followed by base coats of white vinyl paint, then colored with acrylics or colored vinyls and finally spray-on clear lacquer or varnish.

When buying paints, check with your dealer as to what thinners must be used and how brushes can be cleaned. Also find out if there are any special cautions to be observed (that lacquers must not be put over oil base paints, for example).

Bread Paste

A material that somewhat resembles mash can be made out of white bread by adding glue, glycerine and water. To this, water colors are added.

Recipe for Bread Paste: Take the inside portions of two slices of fresh white bread, crumble, add a few drops of water, knead into a doughy paste. Roll it into a ball. Make a depression in the center, add four drops of glue and one drop of glycerine. (This is sticky stuff at this stage—have a container of water at hand for rinsing the fingers.)

15

Knead the mash until it is smooth and free from lumps. Knead in a bit of white tempera.

Divide the dough into a number of small pellets, add a little water color to each pellet and knead the color in thoroughly. Use enough pigment to get the intensity of color desired. These pellets can be used to model small decorative forms—flowers, leaves, ribbons, and so on. When glued into place, allowed to dry, and sprayed with lacquer they are porcelain-like pieces. Unused bread paste can be kept for a while in plastic bags in the refrigerator.

Brushes

The selection of brushes depends upon individual preference, the size of the work, and the nature of the paints to be used. Brushes that have been used for oil paints must be cleaned in turpentine and then washed in soap and water. For vinyls and acrylics you don't need turpentine, but a brush should be kept wet while working and washed in soap and water as soon as the painting is completed.

For gluing, we use a stiff bristle paintbrush. This can stand in water until the work is finished, then it should be thoroughly rinsed.

1. Vases

2. Weather vane (daylight)

3. Weather vane (black light)

4. Block head cat

5. Cyclist

6. Lion

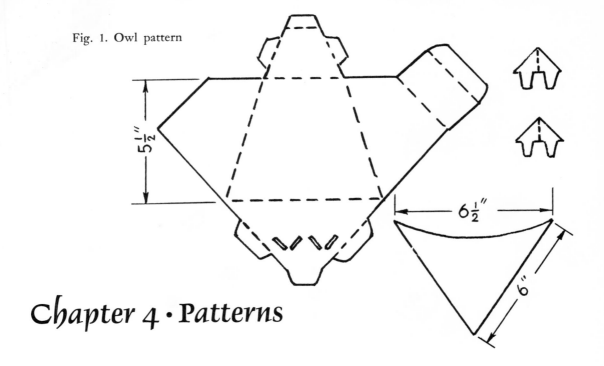

Fig. 1. Owl pattern

$5\frac{1}{2}''$

$6\frac{1}{2}''$

$6''$

Chapter 4 · Patterns

IT is easy to copy a pattern, cut it out, fold it on the dotted lines and paste it together. Things can be made that way. But how much more fun it is to dream up shapes entirely original; instead of copying patterns, to create them! Here is a way to go about it.

PHOTO SERIES 5
Creating a Pattern

1. An irregular box has been formed by cutting a piece of chipboard and fold-

ing it haphazardly. What does this box suggest to us?

2. With a top piece added and two tiny props for legs; it might be an owl. (The box is held together by rubber bands during the tryout period.)

17

3. The box has been unfolded so that a pattern could be drawn from it.

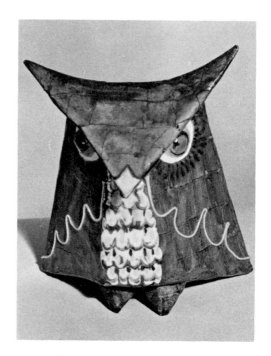

The pattern shown in Fig. 1, like all patterns, is meant to be cut out and folded on the dotted lines. Tabs are provided for gluing the shape together, but the figure could be made just as well without tabs by using gummed paper to seal the joints. The two little triangles with tabs on the bases are folded to make legs, then the tabs are inserted in the slots shown in the underside of the body.

4. The pieces of the owl were assembled and the entire surface covered with rectangles of newspaper as shown in Step 9, Photo Series 1, then given a base coat of white vinyl paint. Eyes for this bird could be made from a matching pair of glass marbles. In this case a pair of flat glass beads (the kind sold in craft shops) were used. These were set into circles of mash. The owl was then painted with poster color (acrylic) and a darker tone rubbed on for texture. String was used to form the outline of a pair of wings. Finally, several coats of clear lacquer were sprayed on.

Well, we have made two things—an owl and a pattern for the owl. In this case the bird came before the egg.

Now that we know how, let's develop another pattern.

18

PHOTO SERIES 6
Making a Whale

1. Again we start with a box of irregular form.

2. By way of experiment we have sliced off one corner of our box. This gives us an idea.

3. A strip of cardboard cut to the shape of a lower jaw and the tail of a fish.

4. It is held in place, and by Jonah! we've got a whale—or at least, the beginning of one.

5. Before we go any further, let's examine the shapes we have used so far. From this outline we are tracing, we will be able to develop a pattern later on.

6. Beginning construction. The joints of our box have been roughly sealed with paper and glue. A second strip has been

added to the underside of the body and the tail to give additional support to the tail. Notches have been cut into the edge of the lower jaw to represent teeth.

7. Perhaps our whale deserves better teeth than those we have just made by cutting notches, so let's make him a set. Here two strips of 2-ply Bristol board

(thin white cardboard) have been cut out and are being glued together.

8. Shaping a set of teeth. The two strips, when glued together, are shaped by being pulled tight around a paint can

that has been wrapped with newspaper. When the glue is dry, the strips will retain their curve. This is called *lamination*.

9. Cutting teeth.

10. The new teeth have been wrapped around the whale's lower jaw and fastened in place with bits of paper and glue. Now, another method of decorating a surface is demonstrated. Small pieces cut

from a sheet of gift-wrap paper are being glued onto the surface.

11. Continue to cover the surface with gift paper. Our whale seems happy with his new dentures.

12. The whale completed.

This whale was made without the benefit of a pattern; its form developed during its construction. From the tracing that was made in picture 5, we can make a pattern (Fig. 2) which, when cut out, folded and pasted, will produce a whale.

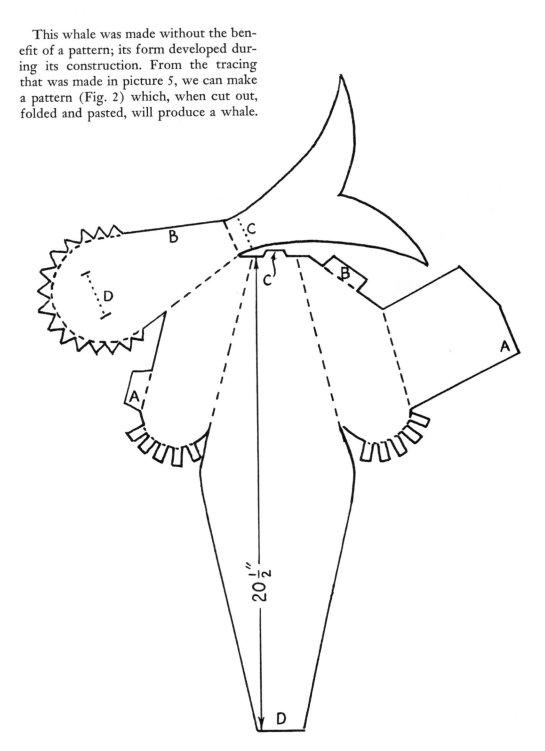

Fig. 2. Whale pattern

13. For demonstration purposes, the pattern of the whale has been cut out and partially assembled. The body was formed by stapling tab *A* to the roof of the mouth at point *A*, stapling tab *B* to the underside of the body and stapling tab *C* to the tail at point *C*. Here we show the strip forming the nose curved around the front of the head.

14. Fasten with a stapler (point *D* on point *D*). From here on the construction would follow the steps shown in pictures 6 through 12.

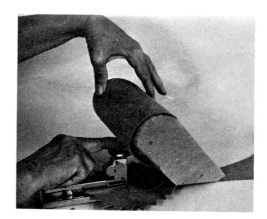

The pattern we have just made can be changed to produce fish of different shapes and proportions. In fact all of the patterns in this book can be changed, so don't consider them things which must be followed with great accuracy. The owl pattern (Fig. 1) can be altered in many ways to produce birds of many breeds. The patterns are given merely as aids in the creation of original shapes.

One of the big advantages of patterns is that a shape can be created many times. This comes in handy when things are being made for sale. It also allows the artist to use many different ways of decorating the same creation.

Chapter 5 · Form

THE work of the creative artist is a search for form. This is true of those who paint and draw on flat surfaces as well as those who create in the third dimension. Form is so important to all of us. We *see* it with our fingers, we *feel* it with our eyes; our whole life is an experience with form. Form is shape, it is also texture; it is contrast (rough vs. smooth, hard vs. soft); it is movement—the flow of lines; it is growth—the shapes of plants and other living things; it is dynamic, it is static, it is functional, it is aesthetic.

As we work in the third dimension, we shall develop a keen appreciation of form, an awareness of its values. Let us start by studying some geometric forms: the cube, the cylinder, the pyramid, the cone, the sphere.

A cube is a box with six square sides. A box may have more than six sides or as few as four and it need not be square, but may be lopsided. No matter what its shape or the number of its sides, any form whose surfaces are planes can be made from a pattern.

Rolled shapes, cylinders, and cones also can be made from patterns. But the loveliest of all geometric shapes, the sphere, cannot; neither can its relatives, the egg shape, the tear-drop, and the various spheroids.

The shapes of geometry are beautiful, and worth a closer look.

PHOTO SERIES 7
Exploring Form

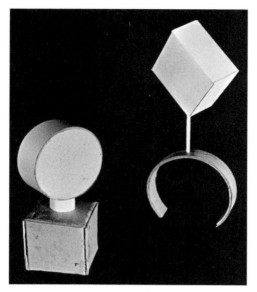

tions, and a rectangular box that has been pierced by a cylinder. The two have been put together to create another form.

3. A different view of the above. This sketch was the inspiration for the piece of sculpture shown (Color Plate 12).

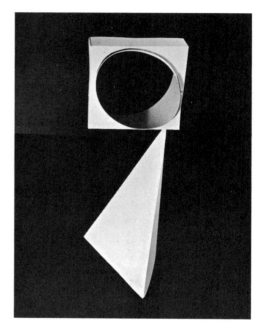

1. We have constructed a cube, a box shape, a cylinder (drum shaped), an arc (made by lamination) and a second tiny cylinder, and have combined them in two arrangements. We have created two forms.

2. Here is an irregular pyramid, a four-sided figure, all sides of which are triangles, but triangles of different propor-

4. Some cylinders are used to make shapes resembling tables or mushrooms. The one on the left uses a section of mailing tube; the one on the right has a column made of flexible corrugated paper.

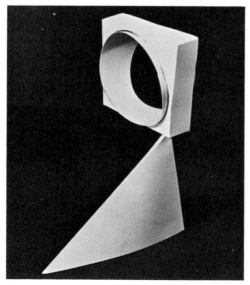

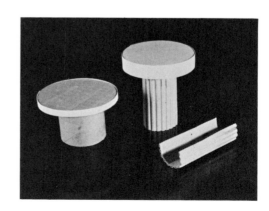

The tops of the two forms are circles cut from stiff, corrugated cardboard with edges made from thin cardboard strips. We shall do more of these when we start making furniture.

5. When a circle is cut on a radial line (a line from the center to the outer edge) and rolled, it forms a cone. Here are some

cones—all of them made from circles with the same 4½-inch radius.

6. The same, seen from a different angle. We shall find the cone a great help to us in many of our constructions.

7. More variations on the cone. Here a circle was divided into twenty-four equal parts and folded back and forth on the radial lines to create the fluted cone shown in the foreground (looks like an old-fashioned lampshade). We shall use a form like this in Photo Series 43.

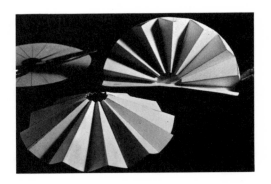

In the background is a fan-shaped ornament made by cutting off five of the flutings and stapling the remaining seven to a semicircle of cardboard.

8. If we divide a circle into ten equal

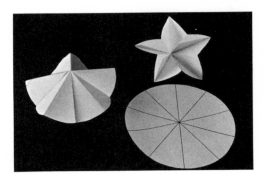

parts and fold it back and forth on the radial lines we get a five-pointed star.

9. Six pentagons fastened together make a dish-like shape with a sawtoothed rim.

10. Twelve pentagons fastened together make a twelve-sided figure (dodecahedron). The support is a modified triangular pyramid.

11. The sphere. No pattern for this. It was made by pressing mash on the surface of a rubber ball. (What happened to the ball? Nothing—it is still inside the sphere. It was expendable.)

Chapter 6 · Cones, Cylinders, Cubes

NOW that we have learned a bit about form, let's put our knowledge to use.

PHOTO SERIES 8
Cone Bird

1. A piece of chipboard that is to be rolled into a cone is "limbered up" by being drawn back and forth across the edge of the worktable.

2. Rolling the cone.

3. The cone has been rolled and fastened with masking tape. A second smaller cone has been rolled and fastened with tape. Here the end of the second

cone is being cut at an angle. The wooden cube in the upper left of the picture has a hole drilled in it just the size to hold a piece of coat-hanger wire.

4. Rolling a leg. Newspaper is rolled around a section of wire cut from a coat

hanger to form a thin tube. Glue is
brushed onto the newspaper while the
rolling is in process, but care is taken to
see that the paper is not glued to the
wire. A shorter piece of coat-hanger wire
has been inserted in the wooden cube.

5. Marking the base of the larger cone
preparatory to trimming it at an angle.

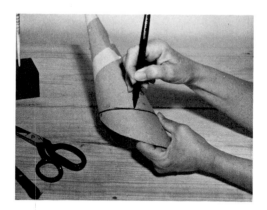

The leg that was rolled in the last photo
has been slipped over the wire in the
cube.

6. A hole has been made in the underside of the body of the bird so that a
piece of coat-hanger wire can be inserted.
Here the bird rests on the wire while a

piece of cardboard cut to form a tail is
tried in position.

7. Fastening the leg in place. Before
the tail is attached, a portion of the paper
tube with the coat-hanger wire inside is
inserted in the hole in the bottom of the
bird. This tube is then attached to the

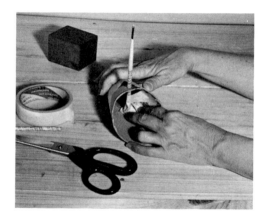

inner surface of the bird with bits of
paper and glue.

8. The leg has been fastened in place;
here the smaller cone is put in place as a

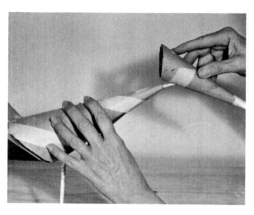

head. Another section of our paper tube
serves as a neck.

9. The parts of the bird assembled. A
styrofoam ball has been inserted in the

smaller cone to form the back of the head. The construction of the bird is completed.

10. Decorating. The bird has been covered with pieces of newspaper and glue. It was given a base coat of white vinyl paint and now pieces of gift-wrap paper are being glued on the body and tail.

To complete the bird, gift ribbons of different colors were cut and knotted and then glued to the top of the head and the tail, after which several coats of clear lacquer were sprayed on.

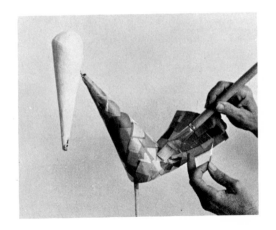

The bird we have just finished supported on the wire in the block can turn freely. This suggests an idea to us—suppose the bird had a different kind of tail, one that was vertical. Would he then serve as a weather vane? We shall see.

PHOTO SERIES 9
Weather Vane

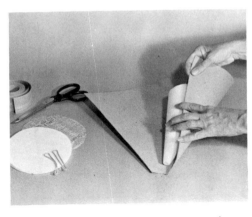

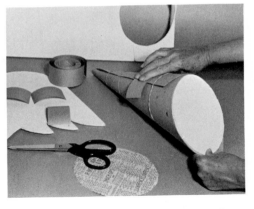

1. We start by rolling a cone using a styrofoam cone as a core on which to roll a 13-inch square of chipboard.

2. The cone has been fastened temporarily with rubber bands. Now it is being sealed with pieces of brown gummed paper. At the left we see a cutout for a rooster tail. This has been cut from a sheet of styrofoam board (core board), a material that is extremely light, yet does not bend—ideal for the tail of a weather vane. An elliptical shape also cut from the styrofoam board is being tried in place in the cone. The pattern for the ellipse is shown in the front center of the picture.

The easiest way to cut a pattern for an ellipse is to fold a piece of newspaper in half and then again in half, and mark with a pencil what looks like the quadrant of an ellipse. With the paper still folded, cut out the quadrant. When the newspaper is unfolded it will have the shape of a fairly accurate ellipse. If it is not exactly what you want, fold the paper again and keep trying until it comes out just right.

3. Making a stand for the weather vane. A portion cut from a wire coat hanger has been bent to form an upright with a curved foot. The foot is being

fastened inside the metal lid from a large jar. Four iron washers are being slipped over the upright to add weight and stability.

4. Completing the stand. The weights have been glued to each other. Now

mash is being built up into a mound covering the weights.

5. A leg of newspaper is being rolled around a long-handled paintbrush.

6. The leg is glued in place. Note that a notch has been cut into the ellipse so that it will fit around the leg.

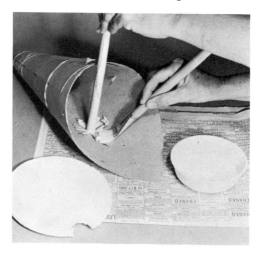

7. Fastening the ellipse into place. Since the body of this bird was rolled out of a square, the resultant cone does not have a perfectly flat base, but comes to a point, almost a natural bird-tail shape.

8. A slot has been cut in the tail and in the portion of the body which is to receive the tail. Here, the tail is put into position.

9. The tail is in place. Two pieces of chipboard are cut to form the head with a wattle and a crest.

10. The head and the crest are tried in place.

11. Balancing. Even though styrofoam board is extremely light, the size of the

tail unbalances our weather vane. In order that it may be able to turn freely in the wind, weight must be added to the head. Here a small iron washer is tried. It was heavy enough to make the bird balance properly, so it was then glued into the inside portion of the wattle.

12. The entire weather vane has been covered with squares of paper.

13. The completed weather vane. We tried something new on this bird and used fluorescent paints in some of the color areas. At night when our bird is

illuminated by black light, the fluorescent areas shine with startling brilliance. Color Plates 2 and 3 show the weather vane in daylight and under black light.

(We have a confession to make! This is a *fair–weather* vane—he has not been waterproofed so he must be brought in out of the rain. We liked the idea of a weather vane so much that we made another one thoroughly waterproof.)

Here is a form made by combining a cube and a cone.

PHOTO SERIES 10
Block-head Cat

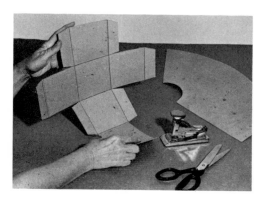

1. Patterns have been cut for a cube and a cone.
2. The cube has been folded into shape, the cone has been rolled and is being fastened with a stapler.

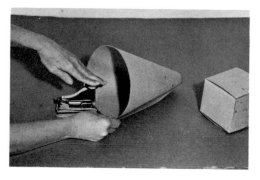

3. The cone is indented as shown to form the body of a sitting cat with the suggestion of two legs.

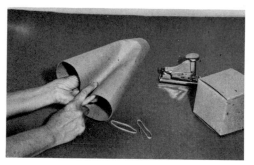

4. Making a tail by laminating four ½-inch-wide strips of chipboard.

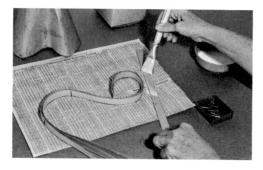

5. The tail has been fastened in place; now a kidney-shaped piece of cardboard is used to seal the bottom of the body.

(Note: where the indentation occurs, the original cone shape will be slightly longer than the rest of the figure. So that our cat may be able to sit without rocking, a tiny portion will need to be trimmed off at this point.)

6. A pair of ears and a nose have been cut. These are attached to the head by means of tabs pushed into slots.

7. A neck is made by rolling a tube out of chipboard and rolling on top of it another piece of chipboard to serve as a collar. The inner tube is just the right size to fit into the top of the body. A hole to receive the other end of the neck is made in the head. A pair of gallant whiskers have been fastened in place just under the nose.

8. The construction of the cat is finished and he is ready to be decorated. The neck has been glued into the head but not into the body and so our cat's

head is movable; he can look up, down, the head can be tilted and turned at will.

After this the cat was brushed with glue all over, then given a base coat of white vinyl paint. After the paint was thoroughly dry, the cat was covered with squares of gift-wrap paper and gold cord for ornament. The finished figure is shown (Color Plate 4).

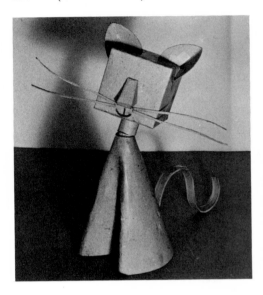

A combination of cylinders can be used to make an animal.

PHOTO SERIES 11
Lion

1. Two circles cut from corrugated cardboard and a strip of chipboard will be formed into a cylindrical body. Four legs will be rolled of squares of chip-

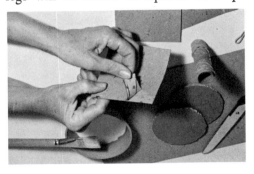

board. Here we see one leg that has been rolled and glued and is being held by rubber bands until the glue dries. A second piece of chipboard is feathered, preparatory to rolling a second leg.

2. The cylinder for the body has been rolled; the ends are being fastened in place.

33

3. The position of the legs has been marked. Now cuts are made with a paring knife so that the legs can be forced into the body.

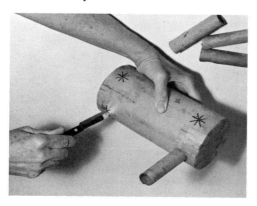

4. The four legs have been inserted and are being held in proper position by rubber bands while glue is brushed over the joints.

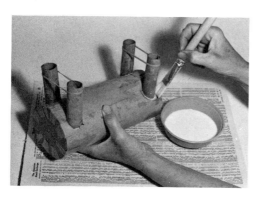

5. Beginning the construction of the head. Another cylinder, a drum shape, is

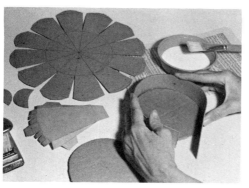

being made out of two cardboard circles and a strip of chipboard. The piece of chipboard in the background cut into chrysanthemum shape will become a mane. Also shown are two ears and a nose.

6. The position of the nose is marked on the face circle. X indicates where slots are to be cut to receive the nose.

7. Cutting the slots for the nose.

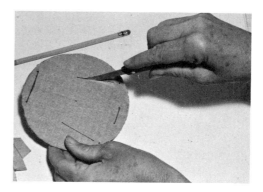

8. Trying the nose in position. (It cannot be fastened in place until later.)

9. Completing the head (without the nose), by fastening the face circle in place. The mane has been attached and the "petals" have been curled in alternating directions.

10. Let's provide our lion with a movable head by using the styrofoam ball shown in the lower left for a ball-and-socket joint. In the upper left we see

the back of the head with a circle cut out to form one of the sockets; now another circle is being cut out of the body at the shoulders to form a second socket.

11. A long rubber band has been threaded through a hole bored in the styrofoam ball (an ice pick is an excellent boring tool) and passed through the body. At the back end of the body a matchstick slipped through the rubber band will anchor it in place.

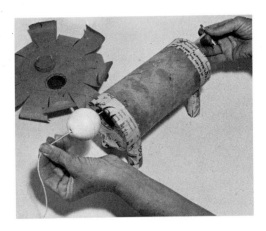

12. The other end of the rubber band is passed through the head. A piece of rope has been added for a tail.

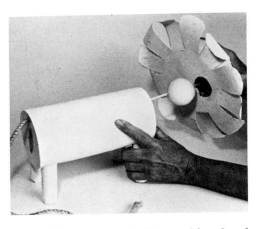

13. The front end of the rubber band is anchored in place.

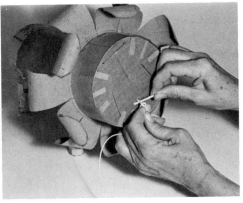

14. The construction of our lion has been completed by the insertion of the nose.

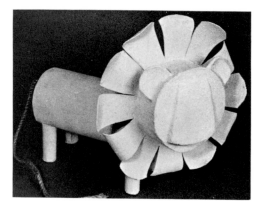

At this point we discovered that the weight of the head was so great that the lion kept toppling forward onto his chin. To counteract this, an iron washer was glued to the back end underneath the tail and covered with paper and glue. The

completed lion was then given his basic coat of vinyl white.

15. The completed lion. After receiving his base coat of white, he was given a coat of orange poster color and then a reddish brown was dry-brushed on. The lion was then given several coats of spray-on lacquer. Shown in Color Plate 6.

We have already made a number of vases. Here is a flower holder of a different sort—a stylized figure of a girl holding a basket of flowers.

PHOTO SERIES 12
Flower Girl

1. The figure of our girl will be simplicity itself. A cone, a styrofoam ball for a head, and a piece of cardboard which, when wrapped around, will form arms, hands and a shawl. The pattern for the pieces is shown (Fig. 3).

Here the cone has been rolled for the body and is being stapled.

2. The flower basket will hold a plastic cheese box. The piece for the side of the basket has been rolled and fastened. The tabs at the edge of the bottom are folded up.

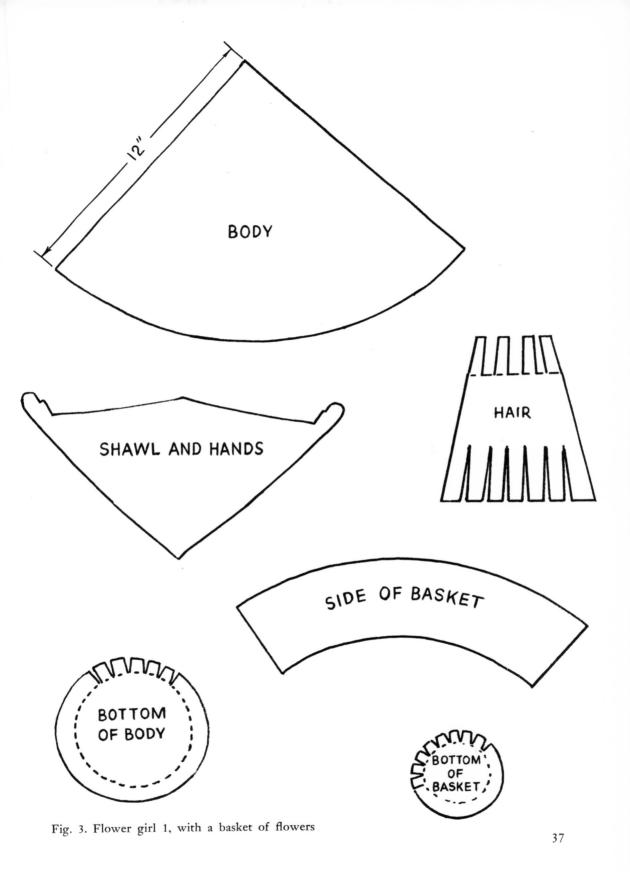

12"

BODY

SHAWL AND HANDS

HAIR

SIDE OF BASKET

BOTTOM
OF BODY

BOTTOM
OF
BASKET

Fig. 3. Flower girl 1, with a basket of flowers

37

3. Fastening the bottom of the basket in place.

4. Covering the basket with pieces of newspaper and glue.

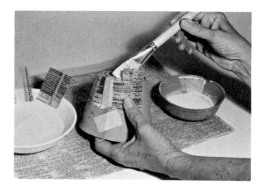

5. Assembling. The head is in place. The arms and the basket are tried in po-

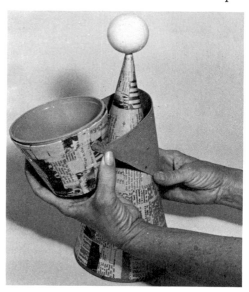

sition. The plastic cheese box is inside the basket.

6. Before the strip that forms the arms, hands, and shawl is fastened to the body it is covered with pieces of newspaper and glue.

7. Weighting the base. A circle of cardboard with tabs will be pushed into the opening at the bottom of the cone and glued in place. Before that is done a pair of iron washers are glued to the circle. This is most important. When the plastic cup inside the basket is filled with

water, the figure will have a tendency to fall forward; to counteract this imbalance iron washers are glued to the inside of the base near the rim. When the base is glued in position, it will be placed so that the washers are at the back of the skirt. This will give our little figure stability.

8. Finishing. This entire figure was given a base coat of white vinyl paint,

the hands, neck and head were painted flesh color and features were painted in. (This with acrylic paints.) The figure wears a black wig that was formed from the shape shown in Fig. 3. The steps in making the wig are shown in photos 18, 19, and 20 in Photo Series 22. Now bits of gift-wrap paper are being glued onto the skirt.

9. The finished figurine holding fresh flowers in water.

PHOTO SERIES 13
Another Flower Girl

1. It was not necessary for us to use a styrofoam ball for the head when we made the flower girl in the last series. We could have rolled a ball of mash,

this way. Here a wad of mash is being formed on the end of a paintbrush handle.

2. The wad has been taken off the paintbrush handle and is being rolled on a paper towel.

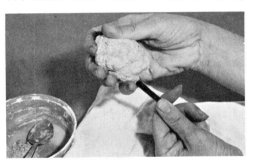

3. The ball has been rolled into shape. It will be rolled again when it is almost dry. This gives it a smoother surface and also makes it more compact and somewhat smaller.

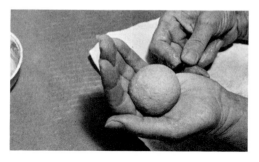

4. Here are the pieces that will form the figure. The large segment of a circle will be rolled into a cone for the body;

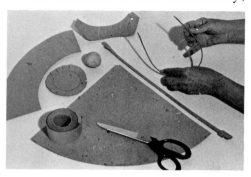

the portion at the top center will form an upper torso. The two long strips form two arms and hands when they are laminated together in the position in which the artist is holding one strip. The head is shown. The circle and arc-shaped strip in the upper left are for the basket.

5. Laminating the strips to form arms and hands: they are tied in a U shape

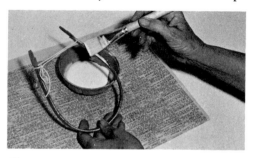

with a piece of string until they are dry.

6. The cone for the body has been rolled and sealed with bits of gummed paper. The head is in place. The arms are being inserted through two slits cut in the cone.

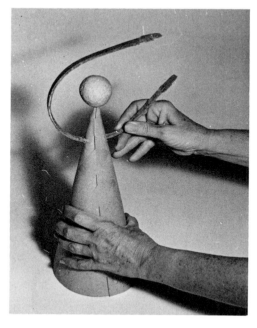

7. Fastening the upper torso in place.

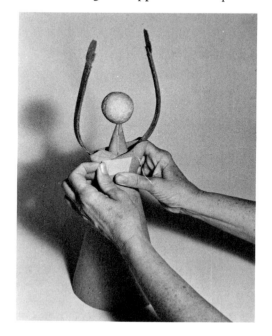

8. Making the flower basket by wrapping the side strip around the cheese box it is to hold.

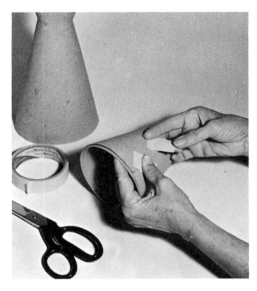

9. The flower basket was completed by the steps shown in Photo Series 12. Here our girl stands on her head while her hands, glued to the sides of the

basket, are held in place by rubber bands. (A dab of glue was placed between the head and the bottom of the basket.)

10. Inserting the base after the glue holding the weights has dried.

11. Completing the upper torso with strips of paper and glue.

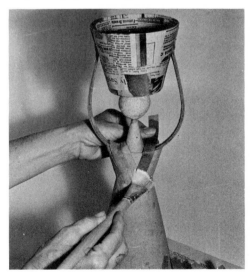

12. Our girl seems a bit flat chested—let's give her a bosom. Here a small circle made of kraft paper (grocery bag) is folded upon itself to make a cone.

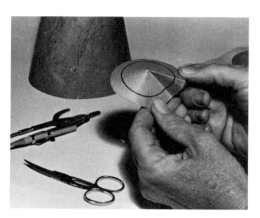

13. Tabs are cut.

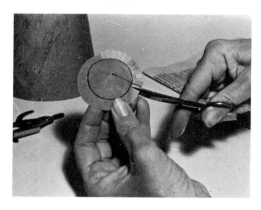

14. One breast is glued into place.

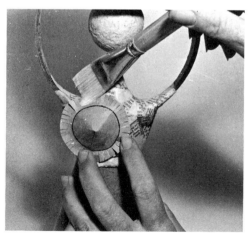

15. The second breast has been glued into place and strips of dampened newspaper are pasted onto the completed upper torso.

16. This entire figure was given a base coat of white vinyl paint and then the head, arms and neck were painted a tan color. Here the hair and a braid are being made of cord.

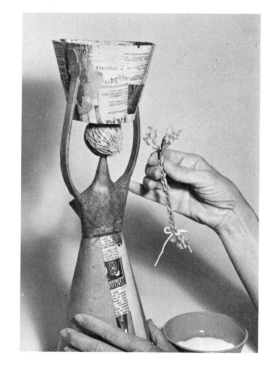

17. Decorating with gift-wrap paper. Two papers, each with a different stripe design, were used for this figure. In decorating the basket one of the papers was cut into rectangles which are being pasted onto the basket in alternating directions to create a suggestion of a basket-weave pattern. One of the stripes cut from this paper was used to trim the edge of the flower girl's V-necked blouse.

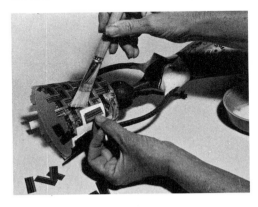

18. The finished flower girl. Stripes cut from the other wrapping paper were glued onto the skirt so that they overlapped at the top and separated at the bottom, permitting the base coat of white to show in between. Another stripe cut from this paper was used to trim the bottom hem of the skirt. In order to make the stripe fit, slits had to be cut in the upper portion. The figure is shown again in Color Plate 7.

Chapter 7 · Balloons

SO far all of our constructions have been based on cubes, cones, and cylinders. Now, let's work with balloon shapes.

PHOTO SERIES 14
Papering a Balloon

3. Glue on a layer of brown kraft paper; this gives additional strength. The balloon must be covered with at least three complete layers of paper (four are better). The difference in color between

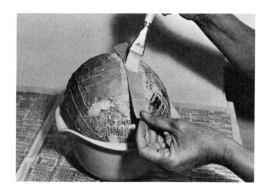

1. A balloon rests in a plastic bowl as strips of dampened newspaper and glue are brushed on. We try as far as possible to avoid gluing the paper to the balloon. The first strips put in place are merely wet paper. As additional strips are added, glue is applied to the surface of the paper already in place on the balloon.

2. Continuing to apply dampened newspaper in a crisscross pattern. The valve of the balloon is left uncovered.

kraft paper and the newspaper helps us to know when a layer has been completed. It is not necessary to let one layer dry before beginning the next one. When the covering of our balloon is completed and dry, we shall have an egg shape. We'll decide what to do with it a little later on. The balloon may be removed by puncturing it at the valve and pulling it out, or we may just leave it inside and forget about it.

4. Ever try filling a balloon with water? Here is one which was treated

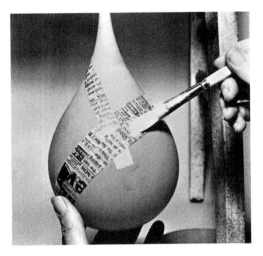

that way to form a teardrop. It hangs suspended from the back of a chair while a newspaper coating is applied.

5. The teardrop after four layers of

paper have been applied and dried. This too will be put to use later on.

6. A variation of the balloon shape. Here we have a balloon which, completely inflated, would be a sausage shape. Partly inflated, as we see it here, it suggests a bird with a thin neck. A cone has been rolled of chipboard and stapled together.

7. The partially inflated balloon has been pulled through the chipboard cone. Here we have the beginning of a bird form.

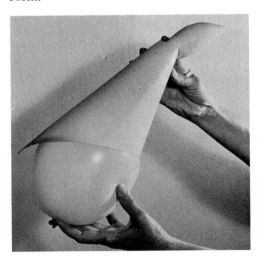

8. Another cardboard cone used in combination, this time, with two balloons—a small one at the head and a

45

larger one used for the body. A piece of string tied to the valve of the smaller balloon pulls it downward and forward, forming the head of a duck.

9. The duck has been covered with layers of newspaper and kraft paper. The string will not be removed until all the paper layers are dry.

made of a piece of broomstick sharpened at the end so that it could be stuck into the ground.

After being given its basic coat of white vinyl, the duck was decorated with a pattern of fluorescent and non-fluorescent colors.

11. Another combination. A long, tapering tube rolled from chipboard is held

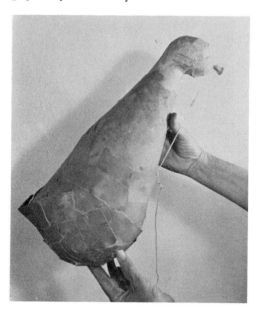

10. This form was later given a coating of mash. A bill was attached and the figure was given a single leg which was

against a large balloon that has been covered with paper. Here is the beginning of another bird of a different shape.

12. The long-necked bird completed. His leg, like that of the duck, is a broom handle sharpened at the end. His crest is formed from coat-hanger wire, his tail is made of rolled strips of chipboard.

Let's shift from birds to animals and make a cat to sit by our fireside.

PHOTO SERIES 15
A Hearth Cat

1. Two balloons, a large one and a small one, are covered with paper and glue. When they are thoroughly dry, a thin slice is cut off each shape.

2. The smaller balloon (the head) is held against the body. When we are satisfied with the position, the two shapes

are fastened together with paper strips and glue.

3. A piece of corrugated cardboard has been cut to the right size and shape

to cover the opening in the bottom of the body. Note the space left for the insertion of a tail.

4. Sealing the base in place.

5. Ears have been made like those of the block-head cat (Photo Series 10) and are fastened in place. Here, a strip of newspaper rolled into a coil is held against the body to see what the size of the tail should be.

6. Beginning to apply mash to the body.

7. Beginning the making of the tail: strips of cardboard are glued.

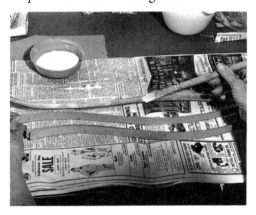

8. Pressed together they form an S-curve (lamination again). Pins driven into a sheet of chipboard hold the curve shape while it dries.

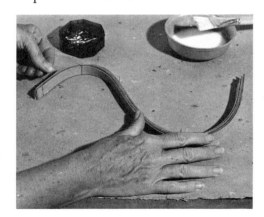

48

7. Haitian flower girl

8. Circus rider

9. Adam and Eve plaque

10. Flower hat

11. Dragon Jr.

9. The laminated strips for the tail are held against the body which has been completely covered with mash. Size and shape seem right.

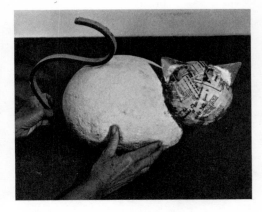

10. Covering the tail with mash.

11. Construction of this cat has been completed, the entire body has been given a base coat of white vinyl paint.

12. The finished cat. He has been decorated with torn pieces of tissue paper of several colors. Black acrylic paint was dabbed on over these with a coarse sponge to give a suggestion of stripes. Whiskers and eyebrows were cut from a whisk broom and glued in place. As a final step the cat was given several coats of crystal-clear, spray-on lacquer.

A balloon can be covered with mash without pasting strips of paper on first. We shall combine the balloon with a cone to represent a head and a neck, and add a hat.

PHOTO SERIES 16
Girl with a Hatful of Flowers

1. Mash is patted onto a balloon. In the background is a plastic bowl in which a cradle of newspaper has been made to hold the balloon while mash is being put on the other side.

2. Completing the covering of the balloon.

3. Using a spatula to smooth the mash.

4. The balloon has been suspended by a string tied to the valve while more smoothing is done. At this stage the mash

is quite moist. Folded newspaper is held against the bottom of the shape to absorb some of the excess moisture. After this the mash is patted gently with paper towels.

5. The mash, now nearly dry, is given a final smoothing with the spatula.

6. The mash is dried; the head is tried in place on the neck, a cone of rolled chipboard. Note how, despite all the smoothing with a spatula, the finished surface is rough. In most papier mâché

sculpture this surface texture enhances the beauty of the piece.

7. Fastening two iron washers to a circle of cardboard that will be used to seal the base of the neck. The washers are glued to the cardboard first, then a ring of mash is pressed around them. After this step the ring of mash is allowed to dry.

8. Inserting the cardboard circle into the base of the neck. The cardboard is cut to such size that it can be pushed into the neck for a distance of about ½ inch. This leaves space that can be used for sealing the cardboard in place and also provides a foot for the piece.

9. The cardboard circle could have been fastened in place with strips of paper and glue, but in this case we find it easier and simpler to seal the joint with mash.

10. Covering the surface of the neck with a layer of mash.

11. When the layer of mash on the neck is completed, the neck is rolled on sheets of newspaper to make the surface smooth and even.

12. Assembling. A short cylinder of chipboard will be used to fasten the head

to the neck (later on). The circle of chipboard shown at the right will be the brim of a hat. The piece of chipboard cut out of the scrap shown in the foreground will be a nose.

13. Attaching the nose. After the nose is attached with glue, it is covered with mash.

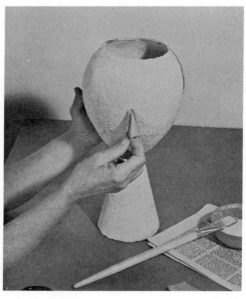

14. Making the crown of the hat. This is going to be a vase to hold flowers so it must have a waterproof lining. An empty plastic glue bottle will serve as the lining. Here a layer of newspaper is

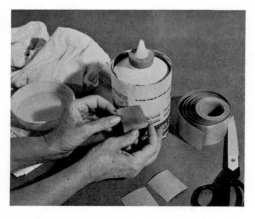

wrapped around the glue container and fastened with gummed paper. This sleeve which is being constructed must hold the glue bottle loosely so that the latter may be lifted out and put back in with ease.

15. Several additional layers of newspaper have been glued around the side and bottom of the glue container. Now

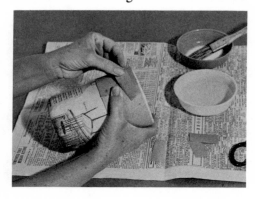

a band of chipboard is fastened around the top. This will make the visible portion of the crown of the hat.

16. Shaping the brim. The head and brim were forced partway into an empty cylindrical carton to give the brim a fashionable floppy look. However, when the pressure on the head was removed,

the brim became flat once more. To make the "wave" of the brim permanent, we had to use lamination. A second brim was cut from chipboard, the two were glued together and before the glue dried were once more forced partway into the cylindrical carton, as shown in this picture. The two pieces of chipboard retained their shape while the glue dried. (The carton is an empty ice-cream container.)

17. The final assembly. Head and neck are glued together, hat brim glued to the head and the flower container glued in place to form the crown of the hat.

Our bit of sculpture has been given its base coat of white vinyl paint. The glue bottle with its top cut off is inside the hat crown holding water and a bouquet of fresh flowers. After this step, face, hat, and neck were painted with acrylic colors; a gift ribbon and some corded dress trim were used to finish the neckline and the crown of the hat. The finished work is shown in Color Plate 10.

Chapter 8 · Sculpture

IT may seem strange to have a chapter headed "Sculpture" since everything we have been doing so far has been, in its way, a form of sculpture. But this will give us a chance to think about aims in sculpture (why do sculptors sculpt?) and to discuss approaches to the art (naturalism vs. expressionism, abstraction vs. representation, depiction vs. distortion, and so on). Also, it will permit us to look briefly at the work of two outstanding sculptors who work in paper.

Dorothy Whitehouse, whose work is shown in Plates 3 and 4, expresses in her work her love for people. She is known for her sculptures of children at play and for the spiritual quality of her creations. This artist works almost exclusively in mash. Her sculptures are built directly on armatures made of wire nailed to blocks of wood. She mixes her mash from a fine quality of white toilet tissue using the formula in Chapter 2.

Patience is required to build a piece of sculpture solidly of mash this way because intervals must be allowed for the work to harden as it progresses. When the sculpture is thoroughly dry, she covers it with a thin coat of gesso made according to the directions in Chapter 2 and glazes it with oil paints. The figure of the madonna has a mat finish; the children were given a final coat of varnish.

The work of this gifted artist is prized by collectors. Some of her life-size sculptures made originally in paper mash have been cast in bronze and are used as outdoor statuary.

Ben Gonzales, creator of the fish shown in Plate 5, has achieved national recognition in the field of paper sculpture. He works in a quite different vein and uses methods other than those of Dorothy Whitehouse. No paper mash—he works directly with paper, cutting, scoring, rolling, folding, and

Plate 3. Madonna and Child (24″ papier mâché sculpture, by Dorothy Whitehouse)

Plate 4. Children (15″ papier mâché sculpture, by Dorothy Whitehouse)

crimping. His creations are highly sophisticated works of art that have been exhibited and sold in New York art galleries. Some of them have been used in displays and in national advertising.

Here we have seen two different approaches. There are many, many more—about as many as there are sculptors. And that is as it should be.

Let us try another approach in our search for form by making some three-dimensional sketches.

Plate 5. Fish (paper sculpture 21″ long, by Ben Gonzales)

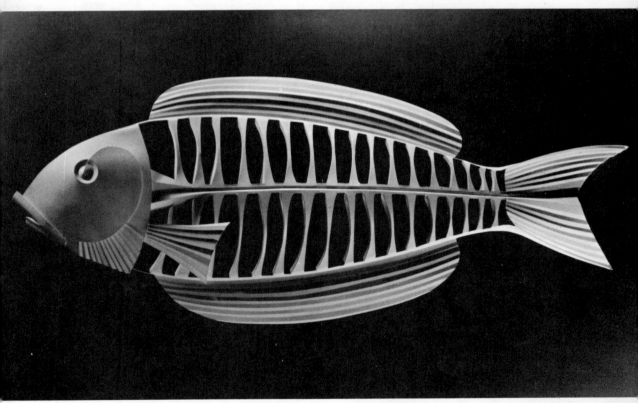

PHOTO SERIES 17
Sketching in the Third Dimension

1. When a piece of chipboard is bent or folded it acquires "memory"—that is, when it is released it has a tendency to go back to the folded shape. A strip of chipboard rolled into a tight ring and then released will take a spiral shape like the one shown at the right in this picture. If the two ends of the strip are now pulled apart, the strip will take the spiral form shown at the back. Curves like these often help in the construction of paper sculpture. We shall see the spiral in the rear again when we start to make a dragon's tail (Photo Series 44). We shall find curves like the one shown in the left foreground useful when we make a wall bracket (sconce) to hold a candle.

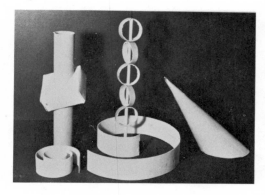

2. Here are some combinations of geometric forms and spirals.

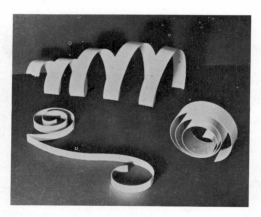

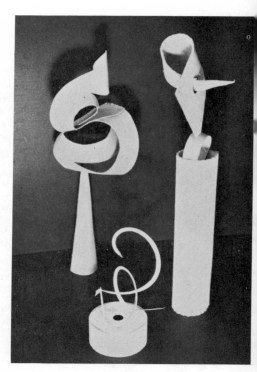

3. More combinations, fanciful ones this time. Do these suggest shapes that might be created as sculpture?

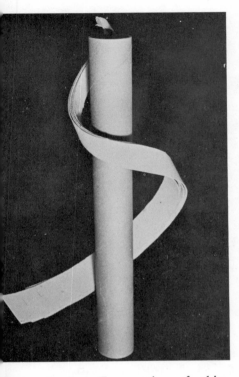

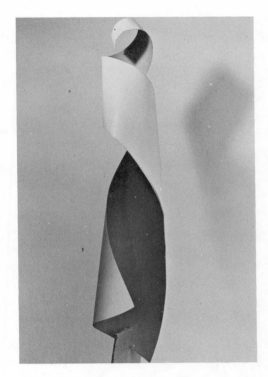

5. A different kind of spiral made by twisting a long tapering strip of cardboard (mounting board). This has possibilities as sculpture. From this we developed the light that is shown in Plate 7.

4. Lamination. Four strips of chipboard laminated into a spiral are tried in combination with a mailing tube. Out of this sketch grew the piece of sculpture made in Photo Series 18, also the pelican shown in Plate 6.

6. A bit of fantasy.

7. More doodling. An assemblage of scraps.

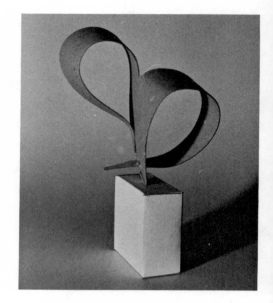

8. Here is a shape with interesting possibilities. We think this would make a good piece of garden sculpture.

9. Another flight of imagination. This sketch, greatly simplified, became the flower girl shown (Color Plates 25, 29).

The three-dimensional doodling we have just done suggests another method: an approach to sculpture by laminating and twisting strips of chipboard.

PHOTO SERIES 18
A New Twist

1. Four tapering strips of chipboard are being laminated to form a curve. The strips have been stapled together at the wide end. Nails have been driven into a piece of plywood that was covered with plastic. These will hold the chipboard in the desired curve. Here glue is brushed on the first strip of chipboard.

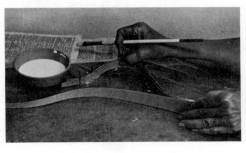

2. The second and third strips have been glued and put into place.

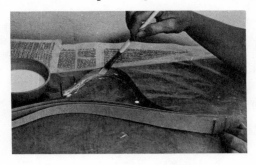

3. The four strips have been laminated.

4. Four different strips of chipboard will be laminated in a double twist.

The strips have been stapled together at one end. A new arrangement of nails has been made on the plywood, and the strips are being put into position. The hammer helps to hold them.

5. Three of the strips have been folded back out of the way while glue is applied to the fourth strip.

6. The laminated twist.

7. The two laminations are tried together.

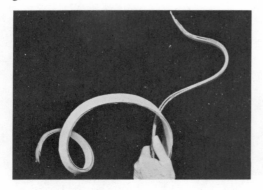

8. The two laminations are tried in a different relationship; this time with the balloon shape we made in Photo Series 14. It looks as if we have another bird.

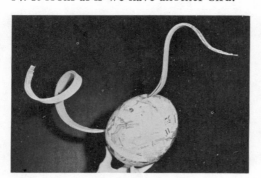

9. Our sculpture has been completed. A ½-inch dowel, 18 inches long, forms the leg; a metal washer suspended by a piece of string is an eye. This figure has been given two coats of white acrylic paint and the eye has been brushed with lacquer to keep it from rusting.

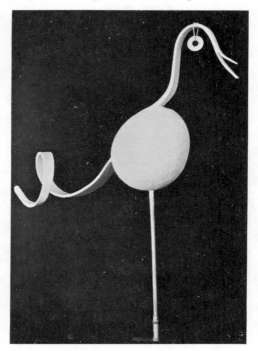

A Pelican

The piece of sculpture, partly finished, shown in Plate 6 was made by laminating four strips of chipboard 4 inches by 30 inches and bending them into a double S-curve. A piece of twisted coat-hanger wire glued to one end made it possible to mount the pelican on a volcanic rock. The chipboard was covered with mash. When it had dried, it was painted with white vinyl and then painted with gold lacquer.

Light as an Element of Sculpture

Another piece of sculpture which grew out of our doodling is shown in Plate 7. Here form and light complement each other. Two strips of flexible 6-ply matboard were rolled and twisted into a tapering spiral, then glued together so that the shape was made permanent. It was a simple matter to install an electric socket in the base to hold a tubular light bulb.

Armatures

Let's take a moment to speak about armatures. These are frameworks made of flexible metal wire on which figures can be modeled in clay, plasti-

Plate 6. Pelican

Plate 7. Sculpture with light

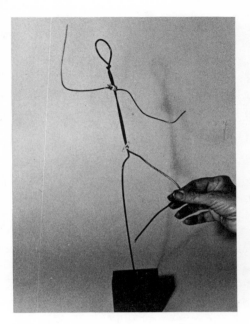

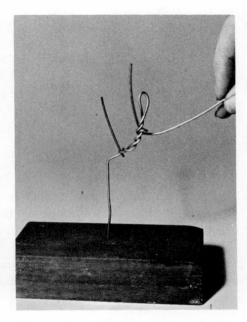

Plate 8. Armature (coat hanger wire fitted into a wooden block)

Plate 9. Armature (aluminum wire)

lene, mash, or any other modeling material. The wire frame may be supported by being fastened to a base or may be held by an adjustable bracket. Art supply stores sell ready-made armatures but it is a simple matter to adjust one's own. We have used coat-hanger wire that fits into a hole bored into a wooden block like the one shown in Plate 8. Regular armature wire made of aluminum, also sold in art supply stores, is much easier to manipulate (Plate 9).

A tiny ballerina 5 inches high is shown in Plate 10. This figurine was modeled directly in mash on the armature shown in Plate 9.

Plate 10. Ballerina (5″ high, modeled in mash on armature shown in plate 9)

When artists model clay figures over an armature, the work must be cast. For permanence, sculpture in clay must either be fired or cast in some other material. In either case, the armature has to be removed from the work.

Dorothy Whitehouse has pointed out that it takes a long time to create her pieces and a long time for them to dry, but there are compensations in the way she works: no casting problems, no need for firing, and the armatures remain inside the finished work.

A Porcelain-like Finish

The arms, torso and head of the angel shown in Plate 11 were modeled directly on a wire frame with mash made of a fine grade of white toilet paper. When the mash dried it was brushed with gesso, and when the gesso dried it was sanded smooth. Another coat of gesso was brushed on and allowed to dry. The final surface was painted with a white porcelain enamel.

This figure has a plastic container concealed in the skirt so that fresh flowers put in water give the appearance of a bouquet held in the angel's arms.

The wings and the halo were made of corrugated cardboard on which a lightweight cord design was applied. This was brushed with diluted glue, then given a coat of white vinyl, and finally painted with antique gold lacquer.

Plate 11. Angel flower holder (papier mâché sculpture with draped costume)

Draping

A skirt for the figure was made out of a roll of chipboard which extended from the waist downward. A piece of old sheeting dipped in slightly diluted glue was molded on the chipboard skirt and draped into the lines of a flowing robe. (Cutting the sheet on the bias makes soft folds.) Pieces of sheeting dipped in glue were also draped over the bosom and shoulders. When it was thoroughly dry, the angel's costume was brushed with two coats of gesso (no sanding necessary here) and finally painted with white porcelain enamel. The angel is shown again (Color Plate 14).

Some Fun: Here is a different type of sculpture built on wire. In this case an armature becomes an important part of the finished work.

PHOTO SERIES 19
A Bicycle Built for One

1. We are using a block of wood in which holes have been bored, and pieces of coat-hanger wire.

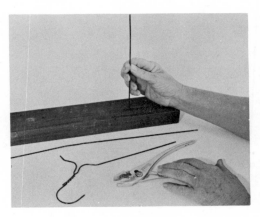

2. Making a wheel. An empty ice-cream carton serves as a form on which to shape a circle made of cardboard

strips ½ inch wide. Newspaper was wrapped around the carton first so that the wheel would not stick to it.

A smaller wheel has been shaped around a glass jar.

3. Assembling the frame. The wire on the left fits into a hole in the block. This wire will form the vertical spoke in the wheel and one of the handlebars.

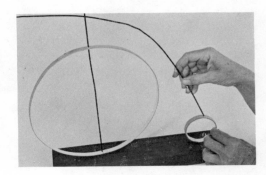

4. Fastening a second piece of wire to the vertical piece. This will be the other handlebar.

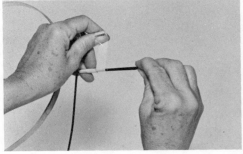

5. Bending the two wires to make the handlebars.

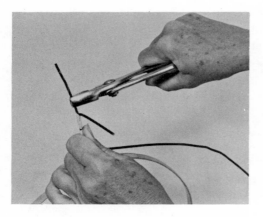

6. Rolling spokes on a piece of wire.

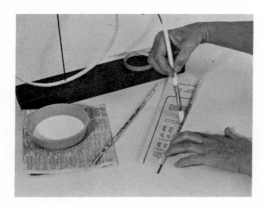

7. Cutting a spoke to size. (The wire has been removed.)

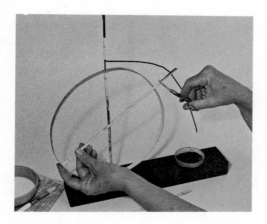

8. A paper tube rolled on a wire has been fastened to the frame with glue and

masking tape. This will hold the saddle and serve as a backbone for the rider.

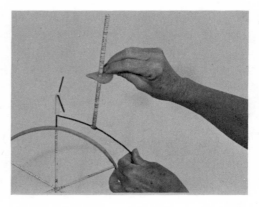

9. Making the rider. His body is a paper cylinder, his limbs are paper tubes rolled over wire. One tube is a pair of legs and feet, another makes a pair of shoulders, arms, and hands. These are not fastened yet.

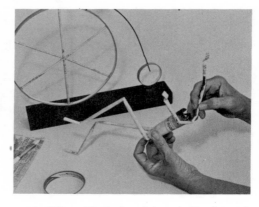

10. The rider's head is a ball of mash made on a brush handle.

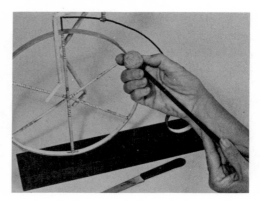

11. The rider tries his bike for size.

12. Binding the rim of the large wheel with strips of newspaper and glue. The small wheel has been similarly bound.

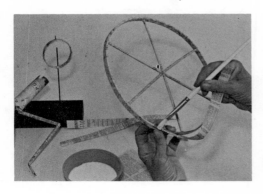

13. Attaching pegs to two of the spokes. These will be the pedals.

14. Fitting a coat (arms have been removed). A tall hat has been made of black paper.

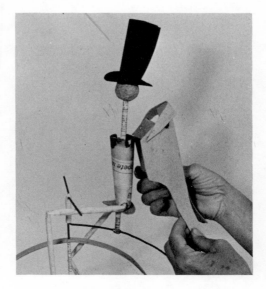

15. Patterns for the coat and the coat collar have been cut out of black paper. Two holes have been punched in the coat at shoulder level. The arms will be slipped through these when the figure is finally assembled.

Here a high white collar is being made.

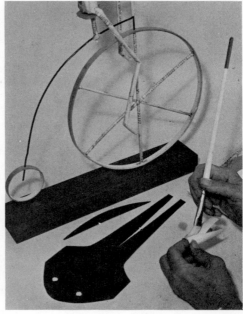

16. The collar of the coat has been attached, the arms have been put in place. Small circles punched out of a piece of cardboard that was painted yellow are being glued on to serve as buttons.

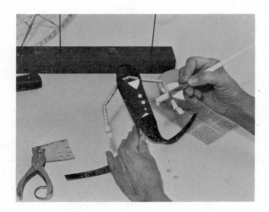

17. Finishing touches on the hat. The brim has been curled slightly, the cylinder that forms the crown has been pushed a short way through the brim. Here the projecting portion of the brim is being trimmed off.

18. The construction completed. The hands have been glued to the handlebars and the toes to the pedals.

The painting of this figure was quite different from other pieces because of its delicacy. A good watercolor brush was used (a slender one with a fine point). Glue was brushed over the figure

and when it was dry, all areas to receive color were painted with a white acrylic. Since the hat had not been glued in place, it was removed until flesh tones, hair, and features had been completed—all acrylic colors. Even though the hat and coat had been cut of black paper, these too were painted with black acrylic. The acrylic colors add body and durability to the figure. Finally the hat was glued in place at just the right angle, a string bow tie was tried—then a ribbon tie. We preferred the ribbon. Three coats of clear lacquer were sprayed on to complete the bicycle rider.

The rider is seen again (Color Plate 5).

Plate 12. Circus rider
(papier mâché sculpture)

Another piece of sculpture that makes use of a block of wood with holes bored in it is the bareback rider shown in Plate 12. An armature of coathanger wire was made so that it could be bent to form the body and the four legs of the horse. Three of the leg wires fit into the holes in the block. The armature for the rider is made of armature wire.

Horse and rider were modeled directly in mash. When the mash was dry, the head, neck, arms and legs of the rider were smoothed with fine sandpaper. The work was brushed with glue, then painted with white vinyl paint. The colors used for the performer were acrylics (a fine watercolor brush was used). Dress trim of gold braid was used for her coronet and bodice trim. Crystal bead trim and more of the gold braid was used to ornament the horse. The "feather" pompom on the horse's head is made of a roll of gift tissue paper glued in place, then cut in thin strips and fanned out. The entire piece was then given three coats of clear lacquer spray (Color Plate 8).

Plastilene

Nonhardening modeling clay can be used to form paper sculpture, as we shall see in the next series.

71

PHOTO SERIES 20
A Wall Plaque

1. The outline of a fish has been drawn on a sheet of newspaper fastened to a board with masking tape. Plastilene is being placed within the outline of the drawing.

2. The plastilene has been roughly shaped and a marble serves temporarily as an eye. A layer of dampened newspaper and glue is being formed over the plastilene. Care is taken to glue the paper strips to each other, and not to the plastilene.

3. Mash is put over the newspaper.

4. The mash is shaped with a block of wood.

5. Completing the modeling. A suggestion of scales is made by pressing with the end of a cylindrical stick. The eye is back in position.

6. The work is allowed to dry overnight. Here the plastilene is being lifted out of the shell made of paper and mash.

7. Trimming the edges. A circle of white cardboard has been glued around the marble to give definition to the eye.

The plaque is intended for outdoor use, so as soon as the edges were trimmed it was given two coats of liquid silicone, both inside and out. Liquid silicone is a waterproofing material used on masonry walls.

8. Painting. After the silicone had been absorbed, the plaque was painted with two coats of white vinyl. This picture shows the inside surface being painted. It also shows a piece of cord that was attached as a hanger.

9. The completed plaque hanging on a patio wall. If color had been desired, acrylic or vinyl colors would have been used and then finished with two or more coats of a marine varnish. This fish, as you see it, was given several coats of clear lacquer.

The plaques of Neptune and a mermaid shown in Plate 13 were made and painted the same way as the fish we have just completed. The trident was made with rolls of newspaper and glue painted with sea green acrylic with a final coat of gold lacquer.

These figures have been hanging on an exterior wall for more than two years. During that time they have been frequently drenched by torrential rains without suffering any damage whatsoever.

Another piece of sculpture made over a plastilene form is the Adam and Eve plaque shown in Color Plate 9. This gay piece was painted with acrylic colors and sprayed with several coats of clear lacquer. It is 30 inches high.

73

Plate 13. Neptune and mermaid wall plaques (outdoor sculpture of papier mâché)

74

PHOTO SERIES 21
A Dragon

1. A teardrop shape is being modeled in plastilene. This material is sometimes a bit tough and resistant. It needs to be whacked with a club to behave as we want it to. Two arms have been rolled (shown between the artist's hands).

2. A tail and a neck have been rolled. The neck has been attached to the body. Here the tail is being attached in place. A spoon is used as a modeling tool.

The dragon has been propped in position on a turntable with wads of clay taking the place of legs.

3. Shaping the legs. The modeling tool here is a paring knife. The legs are cut from slabs of plastilene.

4. Cutting toes.

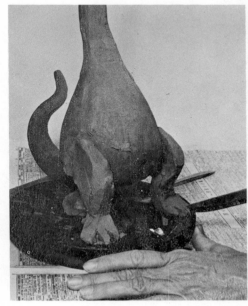

5. Attaching the arms. The ends of the rolls are squeezed between the fingers and then cut into claw shapes.

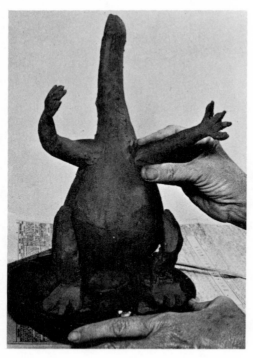

6. A head is cut from a block of plastilene. A knife cut makes an open mouth.

7. Attaching the head. A toothpick driven through the back of the neck into the head holds it in place.

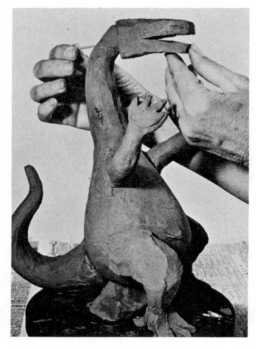

8. Triangular spines are attached.

9. A pair of eyes and a pair of horns have been put on.

10. Covering the dragon with a layer of newspaper and glue. Care must be taken here to keep from gluing the newspaper fast to the plastilene.

Note that the spines have been removed. They will be put back later on. The legs also have been removed. It will be easier to cover the legs separately and then attach them to the body. Before removing the legs, toothpicks were driven through them into the body; these remain in the body and will help in reattaching the legs in the proper position.

11. Covering one of the legs with newspaper and glue. The other leg, detached from the body, awaits its turn. It will not be necessary to cover the toes because claws will be made by rolling tiny cones of paper and attaching them.

12. The legs have been completed and are back in place on the body. Claws made of small paper cones like those already on the feet are being added to the hands.

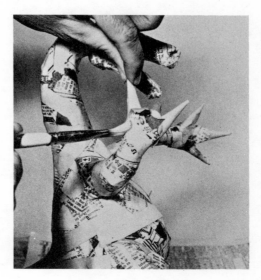

13. The entire figure has been covered with three layers of paper and glue, and the paper covering has dried completely. The plastilene is still inside and must be removed. Here the artist is slicing through the paper shell using a sharp paring knife. In the foreground we see

77

a mat-cutting knife and a razor in a holder. Both of these come in handy at times. The toothpicks holding the head and the two legs are still in place.

14. The two halves of the shell have been pulled apart. The cut went around the center line in the front, through the tail, and up through the head, as can be seen by examining the figure on the left which shows the head and body with half the shell still in place on the plastilene. The portion of the shell on the right has plastilene remaining in the arm and in the leg. In the foreground we see

a piece of the tail which broke off when the two halves of the shell were pulled apart, but this will be easily repaired.

15. It was a simple matter to pull the plastilene body, neck and head out of the shell. Getting the plastilene out of the arms and legs was more difficult. It was necessary to cut a portion off the leg as shown here. The artist is holding one half of the shell and the portion of the leg that was removed so that the plastilene could be taken out. In this same half of the shell, the arm has been opened and the plastilene removed. The portion of the shell at the right has had the leg cut and the plastilene removed. Plastilene is still in the arm.

16. Arms and legs have been put together and the joints sealed with dampened kraft paper and glue. Here the artist is sealing together the two halves of the shell by pasting a strip over the seam where the tail joins the body. The cut in the head through the lower jaw has not yet been sealed.

17. The portion of the tail which broke off when the dragon was cut in half is being fastened back in place.

18. Adding spines. Papering over the plastilene spines would have been a lot of unnecessary work. That is why they were removed before covering the dragon with paper. Now that our dragon is completely hollow, spines cut from chipboard are being glued in place. In the foreground we see some triangles cut from chipboard. The lower portion of each of these has been split—that is, the chipboard has been separated into two thinner portions. These are used as tabs to glue the spines in place. In the foreground we also see a pair of horns and a tongue.

19. Trying the tongue in place. This will not be fastened in position until the final step of the painting.

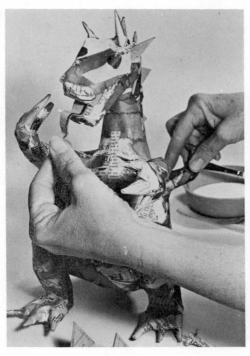

20. A spearhead made of mash is pressed onto the end of the tail. The tongue is in place, but not yet fastened.

21. Eyes. A pair of teardrop-shaped, red crystal beads were used for eyes. Holes were made in the head where the eyes were to be placed, then a ball of mash was put in each hole. The eye on

the left was inserted by pressing the bead, point downward, into the ball of mash. The artist is now preparing the ball of mash on the right to receive the second bead which is seen in the foreground.

22. The completed dragon. He was painted with a small, coarse sponge

brushed with colors—some fluorescent and some nonfluorescent acrylics. On his chest and stomach a double row of small brass nails were gently hammered in and then thin cord was laced back and forth and scrolled at the ends.

The cord, horns, claws and spikes on the spine were all painted with a gold

lacquer. When all was dry, several coats of crystal-clear lacquer were sprayed on. The dragon stands 12 inches high and measures 9 inches from nose to tail. He is seen again (Color Plate 11).

Back to balloons again. The next series shows a combination of a balloon shape and some direct modeling.

PHOTO SERIES 22
A Flower Girl with a Balloon Skirt

1. A large balloon has been covered with several layers of paper and glue and then allowed to dry. Here it is cut into two pieces, the tapered end of the shape the larger. This portion will be used for the skirt of a flower girl.

80

12. Abstract sculpture

13. Flower girl
in green dress

14. Angel

15. Carton table
with wood
and mash top

16. Column table
(black light)

17. Mermaid table

2. A piece of coat-hanger wire will serve as a backbone and head. Two pieces of cardboard cut from a facial tissue box have been fastened together to form the upper portion of the torso. The hole cut in the skirt will hold a plastic bottle disguised as a flower basket.

3. Another piece of a facial tissue box is inserted in the hole in the skirt. This will be the basket. The empty glue container shown in the picture will serve as a liner for the basket after the top has been cut off. Another piece of coat-

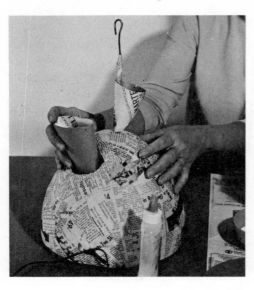

hanger wire has been cut and shaped with a pair of pliers to form shoulders and arms.

4. Fastening the flower basket in place.

5. Sealing the bottom of the flower basket to the inside of the skirt.

6. Closing the opening in the bottom of the figure with a circle of corrugated cardboard fastened in place with strips of kraft paper and glue.

7. Attaching the wire for the arms to make an armature. Masking tape is used to fasten the shoulders to the backbone. The hands have been thrust into holes made in the ends of the basket.

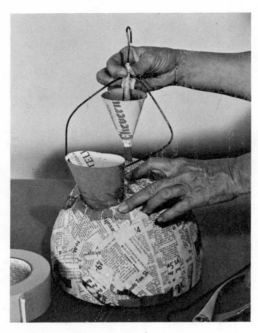

8. Wrapping and gluing strips of dampened kraft paper around the arm wires.

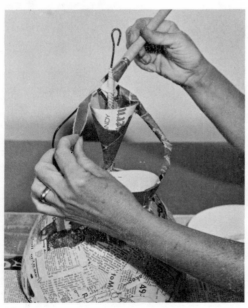

9. Forming the bosom.

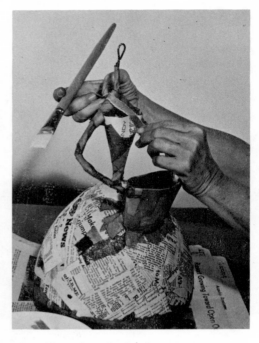

10. Papering the back.

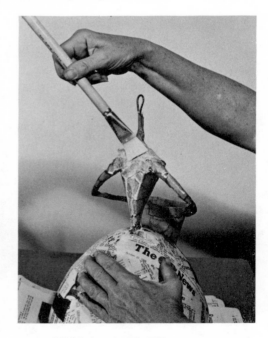

11. Making a head. Wet newspaper is pressed into a wad on the end of a popsicle stick. We use a popsicle stick be-

82

cause it leaves a flat opening in the head which will fit perfectly over the loop in the top of our armature. After the newspaper had been wadded into a head shape it was wrapped with some narrow strips of damp newspaper and glue.

12. The head is in position, but not yet fastened.

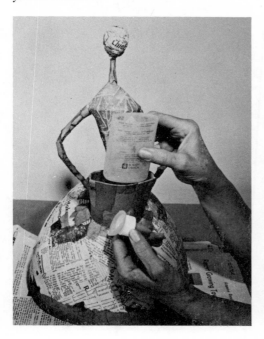

13. Beginning the application of mash. Mash has been pressed onto the shoulders.

14. The application of mash to the neck and shoulders has been completed and the mash has dried. A small rasp is used to refine the modeling. The head was removed and put back on the popsicle stick so that it could be smoothed with sandpaper.

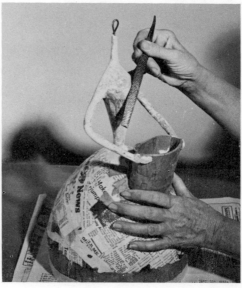

15. Fine sandpaper is used to finish the surface.

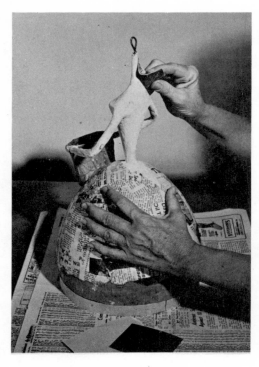

16. A nose is modeled of mash.

17. Mash is applied to the rest of the figure. No sandpapering will be done on the skirt or the flower basket, thus their surfaces will have a different texture from the arms and shoulders.

18. Beginning the construction of a wig: a piece of chipboard is cut as shown.

19. It is wrapped around the head to form a long-haired wig. Tiny strips of gummed paper are used to seal the ends at the top of the head. Care is taken to see to it that the wig is not stuck to the head. The figure has been given its basic coat of white. When mash was applied to the basket, the popsicle stick was used to press a suggestion of a woven pattern into the surface.

20. Completing the construction of the wig: a rubber band holds the wig in place while the ends are curled around the handle of a paintbrush.

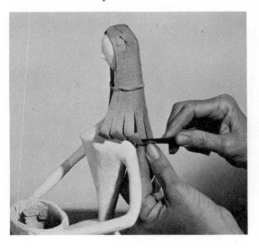

21. Beginning the construction of another wig: the figure has been painted with poster colors. Now a strip of kraft paper cut as shown is wrapped around the head to form a cap on which a wig can be made.

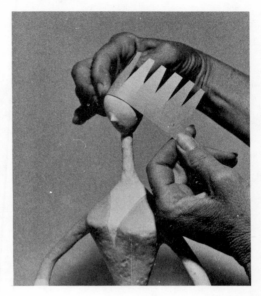

22. Completing the cap: care must be taken to see the cap is not glued fast to the head—it *must* be removable.

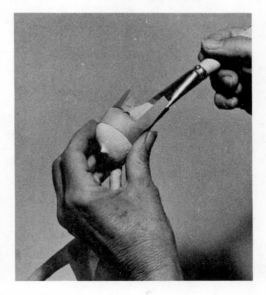

23. A piece of chipboard cut to the shape shown in Fig. 4 has been rolled

and fastened to make a pageboy wig. The cap is in place on the head, the wig will be glued to the cap.

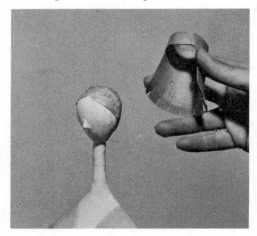

24. A hat made as shown in Fig. 4 is glued to the wig. Hat, wig and cap underneath will be lifted on and off the head as a single unit.

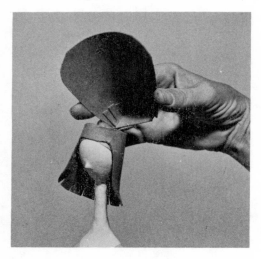

25. The finished flower girl with fresh flowers in her basket. The glue bottle inside the basket contains water. The trim around the sleeves and the V-neck is white, corded dress trim glued in place. A bit of sparkling gift cord has been glued at the edge of the trim.

The design on the front of the dress is a strip of gift-wrapping paper edged

with the green cord that trims the bodice. The rest of the dress is decorated by découpage. Birds and branches cut out of the same gift-wrap paper were glued in place around the bottom of the dress. The face was painted with poster colors. The entire figure, with the wig removed, was sprayed with a crystal-clear lacquer. The wigs were sprayed separately.

26. The flower girl wears her long, black-haired wig.

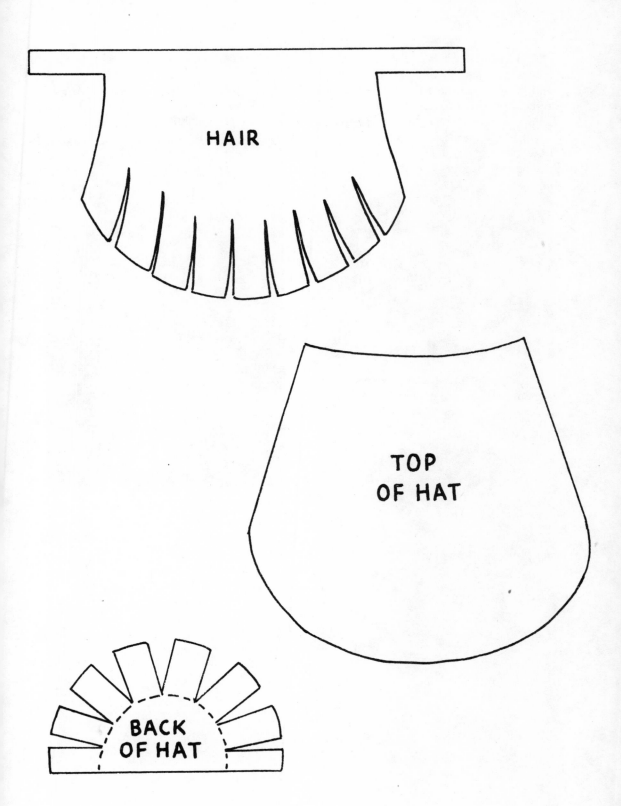

Fig. 4. Flower girl 3, hat, and wig

27. Two more hats and wigs have been made. The hat on the left has a crown and brim in Spanish style, the one on the right, a portion of a cardboard cone covered with gift-wrap paper, suggests an English shepherdess. We can see here how the wigs and hats are attached to the head-fitting caps.

28. The Spanish hat is trimmed with gift cord and a rose made of bread paste. (Bread paste is described in Chapter 3.)

29. The girl wears her shepherdess hat. Her hair is made of red and orange tissue paper modeled into an old-fashioned coiffeur and sprayed heavily with lacquer (Color Plate 13).

Chapter 9 · Furniture from Discards

ONE day at a supermarket we saw an empty carton whose size and proportion sparked our imagination. Perhaps we could make a table from it. It was given to us and we took it home.

The carton was 16 inches by 16 inches by 19½ inches high, in good condition. We tried it for size; its height was just right for a side table. We decided to make a top. Here is how we went about it.

PHOTO SERIES 23
Carton Table

1. Here we see the carton. Leaning against it is a piece of corrugated cardboard cut to the shape of the pattern shown in Fig. 5. This will be the top of our table.

2. Making the top. The corrugated cardboard is folded so that a 2-inch rim is formed. Tab A has been folded in; edges B and C have been folded up and over. Masking tape is used to fasten strip B to tab A.

3. The adjoining edge of the top is folded up.

4. It is pressed into place beside the first corner so that strip *E* comes even with strip *C*. When *E* and *C* have been sealed together, one corner of the table-top is finished.

5. All four corners of the tabletop have been sealed with brown gummed paper. The underside of the top and the sides of the box have been covered with overlapping rectangles of newspaper about 3 inches by 4 inches. The pieces of newspaper were not dampened. Glue was brushed on the area of the cardboard

where a piece of paper was to be, then the paper was put on and brushed firmly into place with more glue.

6. The base and the top have each been covered with newspaper and allowed to dry. This top will not be fastened to the base, but will be removable. This means that any time we wish to do so we can make a different top.

7. The top has been lifted off and the carton painted with a base coat of vinyl white. Final coats of color enamels were

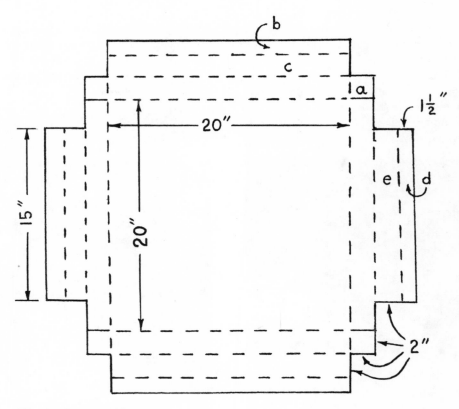

Fig. 5. Carton tabletop

used. The dots were painted on light-weight bristol board with fluorescent colors, cut out and glued into place so that each side had dots in contrasting colors to the base color. The table resembles a die. In this form it would be a serviceable table for cocktail snacks.

8. Planning a montage decoration for the top of the table. Portions of colored pictures are cut from magazines. The pictures are selected so that the pieces cut from them will make abstract designs. These are arranged on a sheet of white cardboard.

9. The montage decoration on the top has been completed and is placed on another carton of the same size.

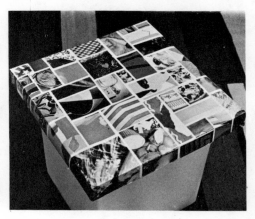

10. Making the tabletop was such a simple operation that we could make several to try out different motifs of design. This top has been given two coats of white vinyl paint. Here pieces of colored gift-wrap tissue were cut out or torn and are being glued to form a decorative pattern.

11. The second color and design of tissue is carefully brushed in place with glue. Care must be taken so that the brushing on of glue does not smear the darker color onto the lighter color.

12. Another petal design in another color has been carefully glued on and now little pieces of scrap tissue that suggested the floral center are glued into place.

13. The table base was also given two coats of white vinyl (a coat or two of diluted glue brushed on first strengthens the base) and then more floral motifs were torn and glued into place on all four sides. When the glue had thoroughly dried, the designs were sprayed with several coats of clear lacquer.

PHOTO SERIES 24
A Carton Table with a Wood and Mash Top

Another table is made of discarded material.

1. Here is a packing case end and a carton that will be used as a pedestal. A portion of a second carton has been glued inside in order to provide greater strength.

2. All sides of the carton are covered with newspaper and glue. Here large sheets of newspaper are being wrapped around and glued in place.

3. A layer of mash is rolled onto the surface of the packing case end after it had been brushed with glue.

4. Smoothing the surface of the mash with a spatula. A block of wood is used to true the edges.

5. The mash has dried; now the newspaper-wrapped carton is being glued to the underside of the tabletop.

6. Sealing the joint between the pedestal and the tabletop with mash.

7. Strips of newspaper are glued in place, covering the edge of the top and continuing onto the sides of the pedestal.

8. Decorating. This pedestal was given a coat of white vinyl and then two coats of orange enamel. The top was painted with an autumn-brown mixture of acryl-ics. Triangles of newspaper were torn and tried in various arrangements on the pedestal base. When the size and arrangement were decided upon, the newspaper triangle was used as a template for the triangles torn out of gaily colored giftwrap tissue. The triangles were glued in place. When the glue was thoroughly dry, several coats of varnish were sprayed on. (Lacquer could not be used here because of the enamel.)

The finished table is shown (Color Plate 15).

In the next construction, a set of wall shelves, we avoid the problem of warping by using a stapler rather than glue to laminate pieces of cardboard.

PHOTO SERIES 25
Hanging Shelves

1. Some portions of the construction have been assembled. At the back is the upright portion that has been made by stapling together two pieces of corrugated cardboard and then cutting out the shape with a paring knife. The corrugations of the two pieces run in opposite directions.

Two similar pieces glued together would warp considerably. The staples hold them firmly and there is no warping. One disadvantage of stapling is that the cardboard is crushed by the stapler so that depressions are made in the surface, but these can be easily papered over later on. In the foreground we see how the shelves will be constructed. At the right is a piece of corrugated cardboard that has been cut with edge pieces that can be folded up to form a flange. The second piece of cardboard resting on top of it has no edges to be folded up; this will fit inside the other piece. At the left is a shelf assembled. The two pieces of corrugated cardboard have been stapled together and the edge has been folded up and sealed at the corners with strips of masking tape. In the foreground we see two pieces cut from corrugated cardboard which will be stapled together to form one of the brackets.

2. All portions of the back and the shelves have been covered with rectangles of paper and glue. Here the top shelf has been glued in place and the joint is being covered with strips of newspaper. A hole has been punched in the central ornament at the top for hanging the shelves.

3. Attaching the brackets. At the left we see a bracket that has been made by stapling two forms together and covering with bits of paper and glue. Strips of paper which project beyond the top and back edges have been torn to form tabs which will be used to glue the bracket in place.

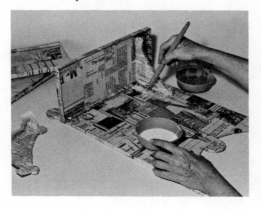

The bracket that is being attached is placed about 1½ inches in from the edge of the shelf. When the construction was partially completed (two shelves in place), we decided that the design would be better with the brackets nearer the ends of the shelves. It was a simple matter to cut off the brackets already attached and move them. This is one of the big advantages of paper construction—when necessary, designs can be changed in midstream.

4. The construction has been assembled. Balls of mash have been formed on the ends of the brackets and on the ends of the top. A similar ball of mash will be

placed at the center of the top, but the hole for hanging the shelves must be protected. The artist holds a tiny cone made of chipboard which will be placed on the top circle before the mash is applied.

5. The ball of mash has been formed on the center of the top. Here the handle of a spoon is used to press in a decorative design.

6. The finished bracket hanging on the wall. Two coats of white vinyl paint were brushed on. Then, the inner surfaces of the brackets, the undersides of the shelves and the back were painted with bright red vinyl. The knobs and the edges of the brackets were painted with gold lacquer. Three coats of clear lacquer were sprayed on all surfaces.

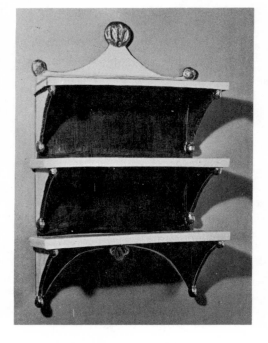

A diagram with dimensions could have been made for this piece, but we felt that it was not necessary. Planning a set of shelves is a simple problem in design. Size and proportions can be varied according to the place the shelves are to hang and the objects they are to hold.

While such shelves are light, they are quite strong—functional as well as decorative. They offer an opportunity to try other decorative treatments, pierced designs in the brackets, and scroll ornaments executed in cord and mash.

Another series of shelves that do not hang, but stand on feet, can be made by fastening cartons together. (Such a construction used to be called a *whatnot*, today interior decorators have a more elegant term for it, an *étagère*.)

PHOTO SERIES 26
Standing Shelves

1. Three cartons of different size have been assembled.

These will be cut down so that they all have the same length as the one on the bottom and widths that vary in a pleasing ratio.

2. Cutting a carton down to a desired size.

3. Here are the three cartons cut down so that when stacked, they make a set of three shelves.

The steps beyond this point were quite simple. The cartons were glued together and one large piece of corrugated cardboard was glued to the back for added strength. Two additional pieces of corrugated cardboard were glued to each shelf and the edge of each shelf was

bound with pieces of newspaper and glue. Four feet were made by rolling cones out of chipboard.

Decorative openwork designs were cut into the ends of each shelf, then the entire structure was covered with several layers of newspaper and glue.

4. The finished piece. It was given three coats of white vinyl and the inside

97

of the shelves was painted with a bright coral acrylic. When the paint was thoroughly dry, all portions were sprayed with several coats of lacquer.

This simple construction has proved an attractive and practical addition to our kitchen.

Chapter 10 · Furniture Design

WHEN we made the tables in Series 23, 24, the shapes were determined by the objects we started with.

Here is an approach to design through the construction of small models.

PHOTO SERIES 27
Designs for Tables

1. A square-top table with four legs made by interlocking two flat shapes.

An interesting design but hardly practical for execution in paper. We experimented and found that this way it was almost impossible to make a table that would not wobble.

2. A round top on a cylindrical pedestal. A cylinder that is quite sturdy can be made of paper. The cylinders being tried are the cores of paper toweling and aluminum foil. By trying tubes of different diameters and varying heights we can arrive at a proportional relationship that is pleasing.

3. Triangles. Here are two ways of arranging triangular legs to support a circular top.

4. More triangles. The two tables shown at the left and in the center were made by upending the triangles shown in the previous picture. This makes the de-

signs quite different. At the right is another arrangement of three triangular legs.

5. The model shown at the right in picture 4 is changed by upending the legs and fastening them into a circular base. On the right is another arrangement of three triangles stapled together. Each

triangle is folded to make a leg containing a vertical angle. Folded shapes like these triangles are much sturdier than flat shapes like those shown in picture 3.

6. A top tried on the folded triangles we have just fastened together. This seems to be a good design. We know that it will be strong. It might, however, have a tendency to tip over. We could increase the stability of the design if we change the direction of the legs so that,

instead of coming straight down, they flare out slightly.

7. To make the legs flare outward, pieces are cut out from the top of each triangle as shown. The legs have been separated and are being restapled together.

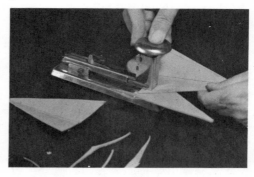

8. They make a table with flaring legs. This would be more stable than the design shown in picture 6.

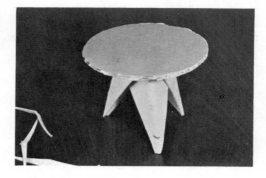

9. On the right is another arrangement of three, folded, triangular legs. This time they are fastened together so that the space they enclose is a hexagon rather

than a triangle like the one enclosed by the legs in picture 5. In order to be a practical design, these legs would have to flare outward. In the left of this picture is another design in which triangular legs were upended, but this seems awkward.

11. Putting the top in place: it looks as if we have achieved a sound design that promises sturdiness as well as stability. We shall make a table using this design.

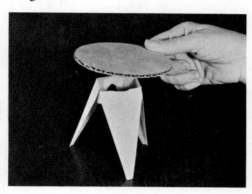

10. The relationship between the legs in the previous picture is changed so that they will flare outward.

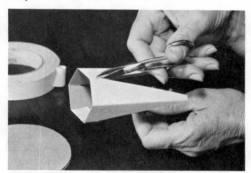

Chapter 11 · Tables

BEFORE we make the legs for our table let's learn how to make a circular tabletop out of cardboard.

PHOTO SERIES 28
A Circular Tabletop

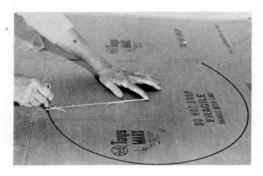

1. A circle with an 11-inch radius is drawn on a portion of a large carton, using a thumbtack, string, and felt marking pen as a compass. A radius of 11 inches was chosen because a table with a 22-inch diameter top is a practical size and also because this is the greatest size that can be covered with a single sheet of newspaper.

If there is difficulty in finding a carton large enough for such a job, sheets of corrugated cardboard can be purchased from paper supply houses.

2. Cutting out the circle with a paring knife. The cardboard projects beyond the edge of the work table during this operation.

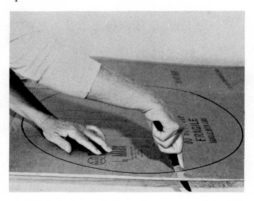

3. Four thicknesses of cardboard will be used for this construction, two of them cut from corrugated cardboard and two cut from chipboard.

Large sheets of chipboard can be bought from paper supply dealers also. A knife is not necessary to cut chipboard, it can be cut with scissors.

In this picture a coat of glue is applied to one of the circles of chipboard. On

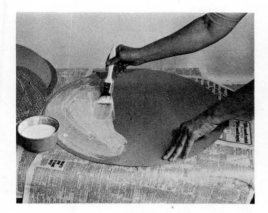

the left are the three circles, the one nearest is corrugated cardboard. It has been given a coating of glue.

As soon as this piece of chipboard has been completely brushed with glue, it and the corrugated circle will be pressed firmly together. This process will be continued until all of the circles are glued together, the chipboard circles on the outside, the others in the middle.

4. A circle with a 24-inch diameter has been cut from a sheet of newspaper. (A sheet of newspaper is only 23 inches

wide, so the circle has a slightly flattened portion on two sides.) A tiny hole was cut at the center of the circle to aid us in putting the circle in position. Now the circle is brushed with glue.

5. Placing the circle. The newspaper, after receiving its coating of glue, was turned over and laid down briefly on another sheet of newspaper, then folded in half so that the unglued sides came

together, then lifted quickly before it had a chance to stick fast. Here the folded circle is being lifted into position on the chipboard which has already been glued. The center of the chipboard circle was marked beforehand. The newspaper circle is positioned so that the tiny hole in the center comes over the center marked on the chipboard.

When it was centered, the newspaper was unfolded and all parts were pressed gently but firmly against the chipboard.

6. Binding the edge. The top has been turned over; the portion of the newspaper which projects beyond the top has been cut into tabs. Here these tabs are folded up and glued to the other side of the tabletop so that the edge will be sealed. After this step another circle of newspaper—this one with a 22-inch diameter was cut, glued, and placed in the same manner as the first one. Care was

taken to see to it that each newspaper sheet was placed so that its center line ran in the same direction. The reason for this is that newspaper has a grain running from top to bottom of the page. When newspaper is brushed with liquid glue it expands and as it dries it shrinks. The amount of shrinkage is greater from side to side than from top to bottom. If the sheets of newspaper were not placed so that the direction of the grain was the same, there would be unequal tensions when the newspaper dried and shrank thus causing the tabletop to warp badly.

7. The second sheet of newspaper has been cut, and glued into place. The artist rubs the surface to make sure that no air pockets are entrapped.

8. The finished tabletop is put under weights to dry.

Warping is a big problem when sheets of cardboard are glued together. The tabletop we just made warped slightly despite all the precautions we took. Fortunately a small amount of warping did not prevent our using it on a table.

A round tabletop could be made by applying mash to a circle of plywood by the method shown in Photo Series 24—even here the top would warp unless crosspieces were nailed to the back of the plywood. We found that we were able to eliminate warping almost entirely by rolling a layer of mash on a sheet of glass and attaching a circle of chipboard to the back of the layer before the mash had dried. Here are the steps.

PHOTO SERIES 29
A Tabletop Made of Mash

1. A circle of glass 22 inches in diameter has been laid on a sheet of plastic. The overlapping plastic is being drawn up and fastened to the glass with pieces of masking tape. (This piece of glass was purchased for the top of another table we are going to make later on.)

104

2. The glass has been turned over so that the upper portion is now completely covered with the sheet of plastic. Mash is being applied with a spoon and smoothed with a spatula.

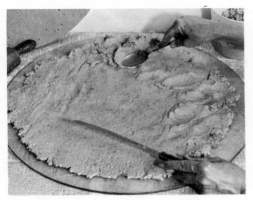

3. The layer of mash is rolled.

4. A circle of chipboard has been laid on the mash and is being rolled to press it in firmly. The chipboard was brushed with glue beforehand.

5. Truing the edge. After this step, the tabletop was put aside to harden overnight.

6. Next day. The glass and its mash layer have been turned over so that the mash is on the bottom. The masking tape was removed, the glass lifted off; now the plastic is being peeled away from the mash. The mash is not yet completely dry, but it is leather hard.

7. A final touching up. After this the tabletop is put aside until it is thoroughly dry.

Now that we have two circular tabletops, we shall use one of them to make a three-legged table like the one shown in the last picture of Photo Series 27.

By enlarging the model we were able to draw the pattern for the legs as shown in Fig. 6.

PHOTO SERIES 30
Three-legged Table

1. Three legs and a hexagon have been cut from sheets of corrugated cardboard. The hexagon measures 6¾ inches on a

side. To draw such a hexagon, use a compass to make a circle with a 6¾-inch radius, then—keeping the compass at the same setting—mark off distances around the circumference of the circle.

The hexagon has been traced on the underside of the tabletop made in Photo Series 29, and glue is brushed into the area.

2. Fastening the legs in place: the hexagon has been glued to the underside of the tabletop. The legs are pressed against

the sides of the hexagon and fastened into position temporarily with masking tape.

3. Strips of kraft paper and glue are used to seal the joints between the legs and the underside of the tabletop. The joints between the legs are sealed the same way and the edges of the legs are bound with paper and glue.

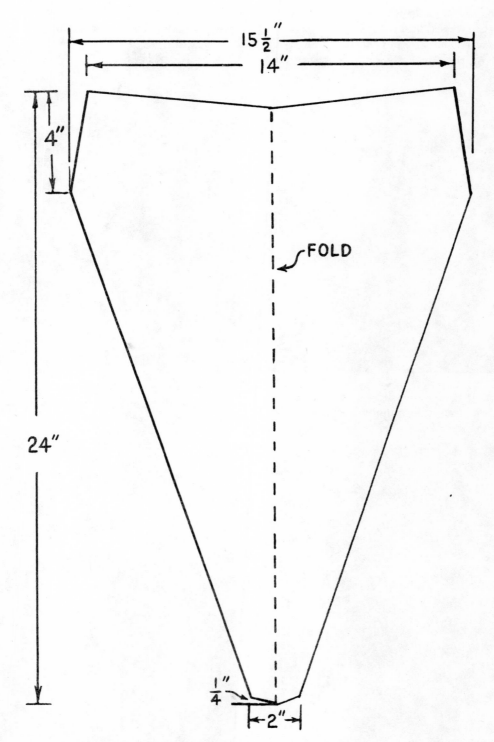

Fig. 6. Leg pattern for three-leg table

4. For extra strength, mash is pressed into the inner groove of each leg. Mash is also pressed into the insides of the joints between the legs and the hexagon. After all of the inner joints have been reinforced with mash the work is put aside to allow the mash to harden.

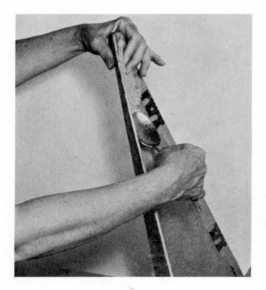

5. When the mash has set, but before it has dried thoroughly, metal tips are hammered into the ends of the legs.

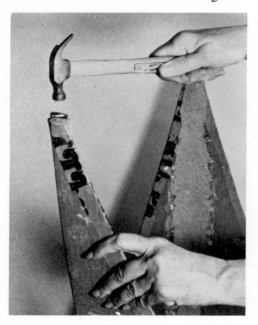

6. The mash is thoroughly dry. All the surfaces of the table are now covered with dampened newspaper and glue.

7. Gluing pieces of paper to the top surface of the table. Newspaper has been torn into wedge shapes; this makes it

possible to cover the top surfaces by forming a radial pattern. Concentric circles were drawn on the top to help in positioning the bits of paper. At this point in the work the legs are damp, too weak to support even their own weight so the table rests on an empty, cylindrical container which in turn rests on a carton. While the top surface is being papered, the legs do not touch the floor.

8. The papering of the top is finished. Here a coating of glue is brushed on.

9. The construction of the table has been completed. All parts are dry now and our table, though extremely light in weight, is surprisingly strong. The model in this picture weighs 105 pounds.

10. The finished table. It was given one coat of white vinyl paint, then a design was painted with black mat enamel (two coats) and fire-red fluorescent oil base paint (also two coats). The top was given several coats of spray-on clear varnish. This table is used a lot and cleaned frequently. Besides being an amusing and decorative piece, it is highly practical.

Now we'll take another look at the little sketch we made in picture 2 of Photo Series 27. A table with these proportions seems to have possibilities. Let's make one.

PHOTO SERIES 31
A Round Top on a Cylindrical Pedestal

1. Here are two large-sized empty ice-cream containers and a tabletop made by the method shown (Photo Series 28).

2. The two containers stood one on top of the other make a good pedestal, but the top is too thin for the base. In order to have a table with the same proportions as our sketch, we shall make the top of two cardboard circles held together by a 2-inch-wide strip (Fig. 7).

3. Forming the cylindrical pedestal by wrapping flexible corrugated paper around the ice-cream containers. Three thicknesses of corrugated paper will be used, then the outside surface of the cyl-

110

inder will be covered with rectangles of newspaper glued in place.

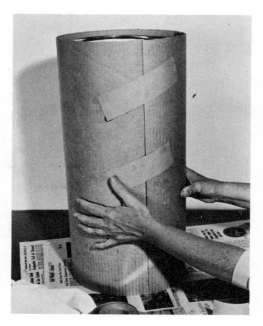

4. Preparing to make the top. In the upper right is the cylinder with its news-paper cover. The ice-cream containers could have been left inside, but the cyl-inder is strong enough without them, so they have been removed to be used in some other construction.

In the foreground is the circle cut from

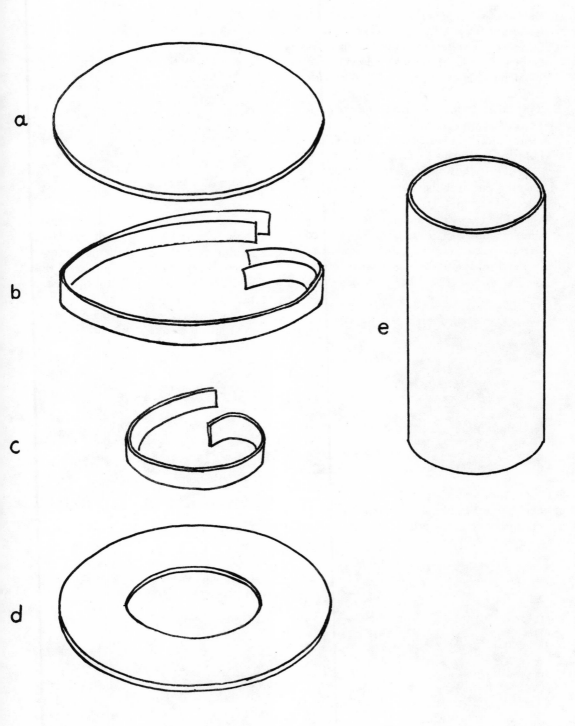

Fig. 7. Assembly for pedestal table

a sheet of corrugated cardboard that will make the top (A in the diagram). Resting on the circle are two strips that will form the edge of the top (B). One of the strips (the outer one) is 2 inches wide and cut from flexible corrugated paper. The other strip, cut from chipboard is 1¾ inches wide. The circle drawn in the center indicates where the collar (C) to hold the pedestal (E) will be glued.

In the background is a circle with an opening cut in it that will be the underside of the top (D).

5. The two strips are fastened in place simultaneously. The wider strip is glued to the outside of the circle. The narrower is glued inside of the wider strip resting on the circle. The joint is sealed with mash.

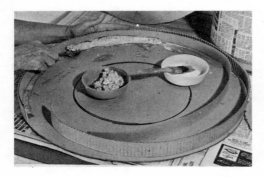

6. Another strip 1¾ inches wide (C) cut from flexible corrugated paper is fastened on the outline drawn in the center of A.

7. The pedestal has been put in place inside the collar. The space between the

cylinder and the collar is filled with mash.

8. The circle (D) has been slipped over the pedestal and now a thick layer of mash is placed around the outer edge. When the ring of mash is completed, this piece will be lifted off the pedestal, turned over, and slipped over the pedestal again so that the ring of mash can be pressed into the edge strips (B).

9. Here circle (D) has been fastened to the outer edge of the top with paper and glue. Now the joint between the pedestal and circle (D) is being sealed with paper and glue.

18. Cone table

19. Chair

20. Head
for bed

21. Chest

22. Bracket and light

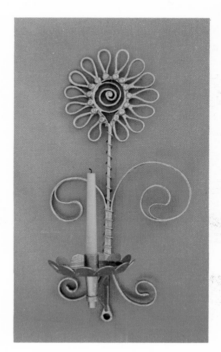

23. Sconce

24. Candle lamps,
decorated with
an abstract montage
of tissue paper,
ssue paper flag design,
a gift-wrap paper
g old tobacco labels.
and a design sprayed
against a stencil

25. Dome light and
large flower girl sculpture

26. Bird cage (hanging lamp)

27. Yard birds
(daylight)

10. The final step—a strip of chipboard being glued around the edge of the tabletop to give a better finished appearance. This completes the construction of the table.

11. The table has been given two coats of flat white exterior vinyl paint.

12. The table was marked off lightly with pencil into various-sized rectangles. Black acrylic paint was used to outline the areas and, in some cases, used to fill a rectangle. The remaining areas were painted with other acrylic colors. To make the table more exciting, some areas of white were left, and some areas were painted with fluorescent colors so that portions of the design would glow under black light at night, giving the table an appearance quite different from its daytime look. (See Color Plate 16.)

The way this table was constructed with a rim holding two cardboard circles together, completely eliminated the problem of warping.

A cluster of cylinders makes an attractive pedestal for a table.

PHOTO SERIES 32
A Six-column Table

1. Exploring design possibilities by making a three-dimensional sketch. Here a number of small tubes are rolled of newspaper. To make the rolling simpler, a cylinder of the proper diameter was built up by rolling a wider strip of newspaper around a pencil; this serves as a core on which to roll the tubes. Seven tubes were rolled and sealed with gummed paper.

are rolled on, serves as a core. Newspaper has been wrapped around the core and a strip of chipboard is rolled into a cylindrical form on top of the newspaper. The chipboard cylinder is glued. The pieces of brown gummed paper seen in the foreground will be used to fasten the cylinder more securely. (Note: If you have trouble finding a large core on which to roll tubes, three or four tin cans of the same size wrapped in newspaper make a satisfactory core.)

2. A circle cut from a piece of corrugated cardboard represents a tabletop. A cluster of tubes forms a fluted pedestal.

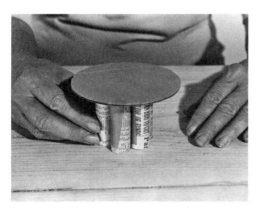

3. The design seems good, so we start to roll full-sized tubes. A heavy paper cylinder, the kind that rugs and linoleum

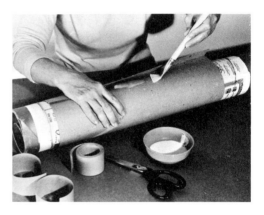

4. The chipboard cylinder (lower right) has been fastened. Now a piece of flexible corrugated paper will be used to make the second wraparound of our cylinder. Here glue is brushed on the inner surface of the corrugated board.

5. The corrugated cylinder is sealed with strips of brown gummed paper.

6. A piece of newspaper cut to the exact size of the cylinder is wrapped around. The newspaper was dampened first, then brushed with glue. While the cylinder is rolled onto the newspaper, care is taken to see that no air bubbles are trapped underneath the paper. Using a towel, the artist rubs from the center to the end.

7. Sealing the ends of the tubes. Circles of the right size have been cut from cor-

rugated cardboard. Glue is brushed on the edges of the circles and then they are forced into the ends of the cylinders.

8. Seven tubes have been tied together. A large circle has been drawn in the center of the underside of our tabletop (made by the steps shown in Photo Series 28). The outlines of the six outer tubes are traced with a felt marker.

9. Some glue to fasten the tubes in place,

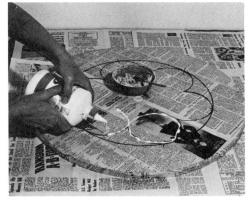

10. And rings of mash as well.

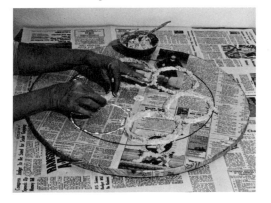

11. Putting the cluster of tubes in place.

12. Scraping off the excess mash.

13. Sealing the joints between the tubes with paper and glue. The seventh tube, the one in the center, is not fastened to the tabletop or to the other tubes. It was there merely to help form the cluster. When the cluster was fastened in place, the center tube was removed.

14. The completed table being decorated. This table was given two coats of exterior white vinyl paint, then tissue paper was torn and glued on in a free design. A bit of decorative gift-wrapping paper was also used. The tubes were painted with alternate colors of blue and green to pick up the blues and greens on the tabletop. (These were the fluorescent colors.) Finally the table was sprayed with several coats of clear lacquer. The top was given additional coats of lacquer.

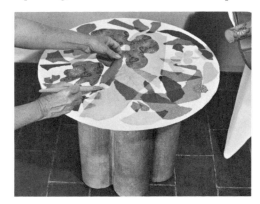

Now we shall see if we can use cone shapes to make a table.

PHOTO SERIES 33
Two Cones Make a Table

1. Two small models have been made to try out ways of combining cones into a design suitable for a table. The one on the left seems most likely to succeed.

Some strips of brown gummed paper glued to the base of this sketch in a modified barber pole arrangement suggest to us an idea for decorating the table later on.

2. Two arcs of circles with the same center have been drawn on a sheet of chipboard (with string and felt pen as shown at the beginning of Photo Series 28). The larger arc has a 24-inch radius, the smaller one has a 6-inch radius. The sector (pie shape) made by the larger arc and the two radial lines is being cut out. This will form the pedestal of the table.

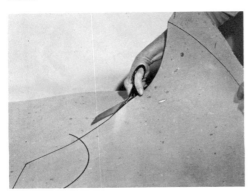

3. The piece of chipboard has been rolled into a cone whose base is a circle with a 15-inch diameter. Brown gummed paper is used to seal the cone. The inner circle that was drawn on the chipboard forms a band that will aid us in positioning the top portion of the table.

4. Two concentric circles, the outer one with a 12-inch radius, the inner one with a 2-inch radius, have been drawn on another sheet of chipboard. A radial line from the outer edge to the center

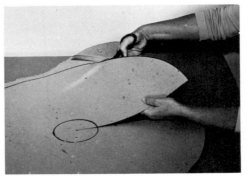

117

has been cut. Now, the outer circle is being cut out. After this the inner circle will be cut out.

5. The shape just cut out has been rolled to form the top cone of the table.

6. The top cone is placed in position over the lower one. The opening in the top cone coincides with the band on the larger cone.

7. Sealing the joints between the two cones with strips of kraft paper and glue. After this step was completed the entire outer surface of both cones was covered with newspaper and glue.

8. The two cones are fastened together. The outer edge of the top cone has been bound with pieces of kraft paper and glue and rectangles of newspaper have been pasted on the inside for extra strength.

A cylinder rolled of flexible corrugated paper is being fastened around the point of the lower cone. This cylinder must be just high enough so that it will support the top surface of the table. Mash is being pressed around the base of the cylinder to hold it firmly in place. The work must be allowed to dry before the next step is undertaken.

9. A circular tabletop has been made by the steps shown in Photo Series 28. The outer edge of the circle has been ringed with mash and a smaller ring of mash, with the same diameter as the cylinder shown in photo 8, has been made in the center. The assembled portion of the table, which by now is dry, is lifted up and put into place on the

underside of the cardboard top, then pressed firmly into place.

10. Finishing the edge of the top portion with mash.

11. A circle of corrugated cardboard is fastened inside of the taller cone to seal the opening in the base.

12. The construction must now be allowed to dry for a day or two. Some large books piled on the base serve as weights pressing all the parts of the assembled table firmly together.

13. After the table was dry a layer of mash was spread on the top and smoothed with a spatula. Here mash is applied to the outer surface of the table and patted into place with a brush.

14. All surfaces of the table have been covered with mash; the construction is now complete. The entire table has been given two coats of exterior white vinyl paint.

15. Decorating. The stripes on the pedestal of the model we made in photo 1 suggest a patriotic motif. Here strips of 2-inch-wide masking tape are wrapped around the pedestal so that the spaces between them are exactly 2 inches wide. A compass helps in placing the strips.

16. Preparing to decorate the top. Strips of masking tape were fastened over the entire top, then stars were
120

drawn on the tape with a felt pen. The edges of the stars were then cut with a razor blade and the tape between the stars was pulled away. The same thing was done to the under surface of the upper cone.

17. The spaces between the strips of tape on the pedestal were painted bright red. When the paint was thoroughly dry the strips of tape were peeled away as shown here, leaving a pattern of red and white stripes.

The portion between the stars was painted blue. When the tape that formed

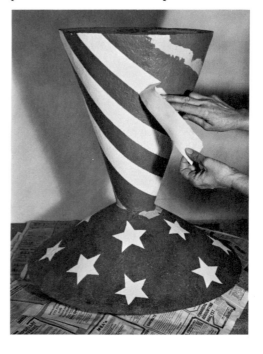

the stars was peeled away, the stars were white on a blue field.

18. The completed table. This view shows the design made by the stripes on the other side of the pedestal. The blue and the red paints used were acrylics. Finally, several coats of crystal-clear lacquer were sprayed on. The top surface of the table received a few extra coats of the spray. (This table is shown again in Color Plate 18.)

Chapter 12 · Tables with Glass Tops

A COMPLETELY different kind of table can be made by using a papier mâché construction to support a glass top. In such a table the important part of the design is what is seen when one looks downward through the glass at the supporting construction.

PHOTO SERIES 34
A Flower-Petal Table

1. Again we make a small model. Four modified cylindrical forms cut into shapes resembling flower petals are held in slots made in a circular disc.

2. The sketch has been enlarged and made full size. The pattern is an attractive one, but it proved difficult to construct. In the course of making the table this design was modified, as we shall see later on.

3. The piece of glass that we used in Photo Series 29 will be the top of our table. Here a strip of chipboard, 1 inch wide, is being wrapped around the glass to form a rim.

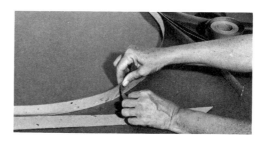

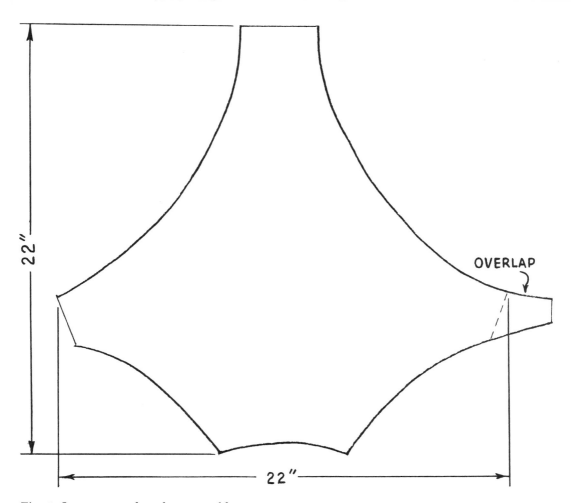

Fig. 8. Leg pattern for glass-top table

4. A second strip of chipboard ¾ inch wide is glued inside the first strip. This second strip rests on the glass (newspaper prevents the strip from being glued fast to the glass). Since the thickness of the glass is ¼ inch, the top edges of these two strips will be even.

After this step is completed an additional strip of chipboard was fastened around the outer edge.

5. Shapes for the legs have been cut out according to the pattern shown in Fig. 8. The shapes are rolled into tubular form and fastened with a stapler.

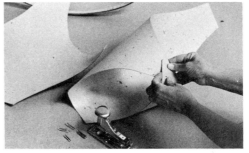

6. A small cylinder 2½ inches high and 2½ inches in diameter (to serve as a connecting core) has been made out of chipboard. The four legs of the table are assembled by being tied to the core. Paper clips are used to fasten the legs to each other.

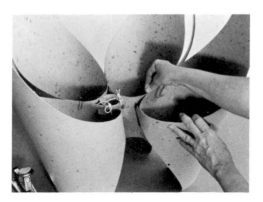

This change in design made the construction easier and sturdier, and also improved the table's appearance.

7. The last leg is tied in place.

8. The leg assembly is fastened to the rim of the table. Each leg has been sta-

pled to the inside of the rim. Here an additional strip of chipboard ¾ inches wide is stapled inside the rim. This strip covers the ends of the legs.

9. For extra strength an additional piece of chipboard is inserted in each of the legs. This is glued in place.

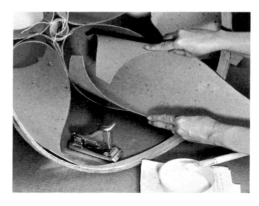

10. After the legs have been reinforced the table construction is placed upside down on the glass and a coating of mash is applied to the outer surfaces. Mash is also pressed into the crevices where the legs join. During this operation the leg assembly is supported by a cardboard tube that rests on the glass.

11. Gluing pieces of paper onto the rim. The bits of paper are 2 inches wide and 3 inches or 4 inches long. Tears are made from the top of each strip to the center. When the strips are attached they are glued to the outer edge of the rim.

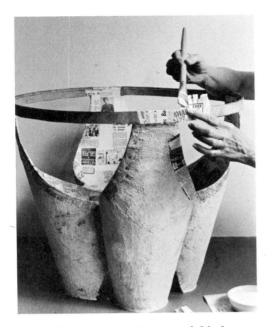

12. The torn portions are folded over and glued to the inner side. Care must be taken here to see that the pieces fit neatly into the groove which is going to hold the glass.

13. The construction is completed, the table has been assembled and the glass is in place. We are now ready to paint.

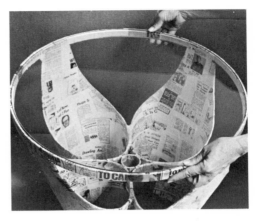

14. Decorating. After the table had been given two coats of white vinyl paint, the inside surfaces of the legs were painted with bright pink fluorescent paint. The outside surfaces were painted with yellow vinyl paint. The rim was painted with black acrylic paint.

The cord design on the inside of the legs was drawn on a page of newspaper. A sheet of plastic was laid over the drawing and an ornament was made of medium-weight cord and glue, held in place by pins until the glue dried.

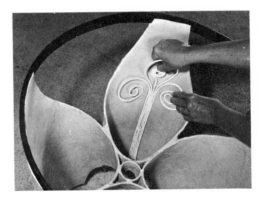

After the pins were taken out the design was painted with white acrylic paint. When the paint was dry, the ornament was lifted off the plastic sheet, and bits of glue and paint were trimmed from the edges. Four ornaments were made this way and glued to the insides of the legs. The cylinder in the center holds a small plastic cup with a bouquet.

When a glass top is used for a table, a sculptured figure frequently makes an attractive support.

PHOTO SERIES 35
A Mermaid Table

1. A sketch of a mermaid is modeled in plastilene. The mermaid is in such a position that her hands and her tail would be able to support a glass disc.

2. A ring to represent a circle of glass is tried on the plastilene figure. The design seems pleasing. We shall proceed with the construction.

3. Starting to build a framework for the figure. Two cones have been fastened to a circle of corrugated cardboard which will serve as a temporary base. The one on the right will be the tail, the one on the left will support the chest, arms and head. The cone in the lower left will be used for chest and shoulders. Tubes at right will be arms. (All of these are made of chipboard.)

126

In the center rear is a shape made by gluing paper over a balloon. This will be the head.

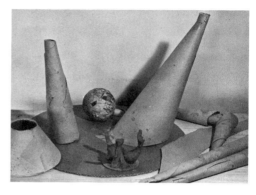

4. A short tube of chipboard has been inserted in the head. Here the head is being attached to the neck. The cone that will form the chest and shoulders is in place.

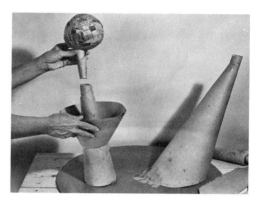

5. A strip of chipboard will form the waist.

6. Arms are put in place.

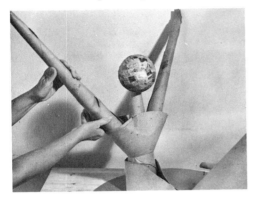

7. A circle of glass 28 inches in diameter will be used for the top of the table. A temporary rim made of strips of chipboard was formed around the glass by the method used in picture 3 and 4 of Photo Series 34. Here the rim has been fastened to the hands.

Two chipboard cones that will form the end of the tail are being attached.

8. Tying the construction together. The cone forming the tail has been bent

into a more fish-like shape. (One of the advantages of using chipboard to build a core is that it can be changed so easily by cutting or bending.)

9. At this point it was found necessary to construct a temporary supporting frame. A circle of plywood cut to the same diameter as the glass we are going to use has been placed under the construction and four temporary legs to hold the rim in position. The tubes are all the same length. Since one end of each tube rests on the plywood and the other end is fastened to the rim, we can be sure that the rim is being held level.

Here, strips of chipboard are used to model a tail with flowing lines. Since the tail will support the glass, the ends of the tail strips are tied to the tabletop rim.

10. A piece of chipboard, cut and stapled to form a pair of hips and buttocks, is fastened in place temporarily by being pinned to the bottom circle of corrugated cardboard.

11. The arms will need extra strength to hold up the glass. Extra pieces of chipboard, cut and folded as shown at the left, will be wrapped around the underside of the arms to give them extra reinforcement.

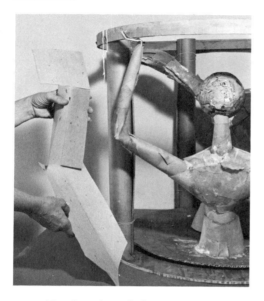

12. Putting the reinforcement in place on the arm. The lower end projects downward far enough so that it can be fastened to the main supporting cone. After this, pieces of string are tied around the arms.

13. A piece of chipboard cut, folded and stapled to form the upper portion of

the torso is fastened in place with strips of gummed paper.

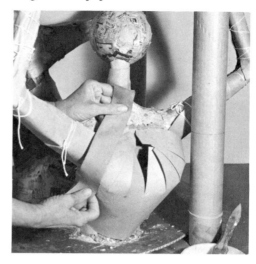

14. The strip forming the upper portion of the torso is pulled around the figure and fastened in back. Following this step, strips of newspaper and glue are fastened over all the important joinings and used wherever it is necessary to fill out forms before the application of mash. Then the construction is allowed to dry.

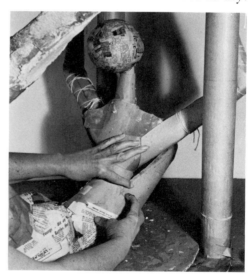

15. After the framework is dry, the supporting columns and the temporary rim are removed so that the figure can be covered with mash. Here mash is ap-

plied with a spoon and a paintbrush. Anatomic details are modeled as the mash is pressed onto the framework. We did not forget to brush glue on the framework before applying the mash.

16. The coating of mash is partially completed. The glass top is being tried in place. At this point a spirit level was used to make sure that the mermaid was holding the glass absolutely level. Any necessary adjustments could be made at this stage by adding bits of mash at the support points.

The temporary circular base of corrugated cardboard will be removed when the figure is finished. To take its place, an additional area of support must be provided at the front of the figure. This will be done by giving the mermaid long, flowing hair. Here a wig made of chipboard has been placed in temporary position on the head. The ends of the wig are shown extending downward and outward onto the temporary base.

17. The wig has been removed while facial features are modeled. After this step the wig was glued to the head and covered with mash which was modeled into the lines of flowing hair.

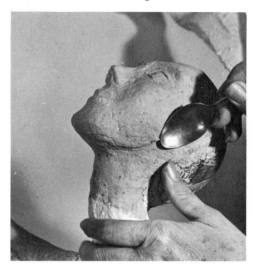

18. The modeling has been completed, the base removed, the figure has been given its base coat of white vinyl paint. After this, bright green and aqua acrylic paint were dabbed over the body with a sponge. Orange vermilion was dabbed on the hair. Then the entire figure was painted with gold lacquer. The rough texture allowed bits of color to show through the gold. When the gold was dry, several coats of clear lacquer were sprayed over the entire figure. The finished work is seen in Color Plate 17.

Chapter 13 · A Headboard

OTHER articles of furniture can be made at times by combining paper construction with wood. We were able to convert the end of a discarded packing case into a headboard in Spanish Colonial style (antique white with gold ornamentation) by using an adaptation of a design motif that we found on a Spanish Colonial bench. Here are the steps:

PHOTO SERIES 36
A Headboard for a Bed

1. A design was sketched in a notebook (Fig. 9), then enlarged to full scale by the method of squaring.

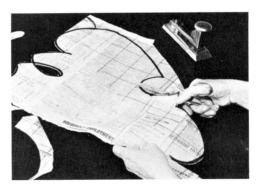

2. The outline of the enlarged drawing is cut out to make a pattern.

3. The pattern has been fastened to the piece of plywood. Here the outline of the pattern is being traced. Before we undertook the next step we had to have help from a friend—it was necessary to have a saber saw to cut the plywood to the outline of the pattern we have just traced. Our friend, who owns such a saw, cut it for us. Otherwise we could have had the outline cut at any cabinet or woodworking shop.

Fig. 9. Sketch for headboard

4. The outline of the headboard has been cut out, and 1-inch by 2-inch wooden strips have been nailed on the back of the plywood for reinforcing and to keep the plywood from warping. The tendency of the plywood to warp was so strong, that we used oversized nails, hammered them all the way through and then bent the ends back into the face.

131

The piece of plywood was 2 inches narrower than the width of the bed for which the headboard was intended, so when it was nailed to the supporting frame seen here, each of the side pieces of the frame projected 1 inch beyond the plywood.

5. The next step—cover all surfaces of the headboard with squares of newspaper and glue. This was necessary to cover a number of knots, rough places, and also the nail points which had been bent into the face of the headboard. The surface

was so uneven that one layer of newspaper was not enough. We used several layers of kraft paper and newspaper.

The area where the frame projects beyond the plywood (as mentioned in Step 4) is being filled with mash.

6. Ornamentation. The design planned in the sketch is executed as a raised decoration by gluing on heavy cord. The

132

cord and the plywood were so tough that a small hammer had to be used to force the pins through the cord into the plywood while the glue hardened.

7. Balls of mash are put in place and smoothed with a paring knife. Leaf designs of mash have been placed and smaller balls of mash have been attached to the ornament seen in the upper right. After the bits of mash were put in position, the end of a paintbrush was pressed into each one. (The pins holding the cord were pulled out with pliers. It is important to press the cord down firmly with the thumb or a fork when the pins are pulled out.)

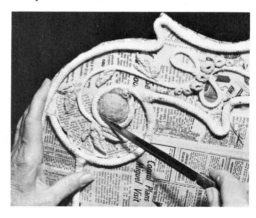

8. The ornamentation has been finished and the entire headboard has been given two coats of white vinyl paint. After this had dried, a coat of porcelain-white enamel was brushed on.

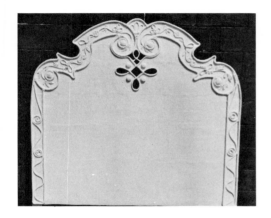

9. A detail view of the center ornament. A portion of the design has received its first coat of ready-mixed gold paint.

After this step, acrylic paint—raw umber and burnt sienna—mixed in equal parts and thinned with water was applied to small areas, then wiped lightly with paper toweling. When the desired effect of antiquing was acquired, the ornamentation was given its final coat of gold paint (Color Plate 20).

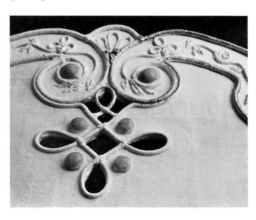

Chapter 14 · Refurbishing Old Furniture

THE techniques of papier mâché and cord decoration can be used to salvage a piece of furniture that is too delapidated to be rescued in any other way. Plate 14 shows a desk which had been thrown away—its surface was beyond repair by any of the usual ways of refinishing furniture. However, it was covered with layers of newspaper and glue. (The surface was so badly marred that four complete layers were needed.) A decorative pattern of

Plate 14. Desk refinished with paper and cord, by Harvel Turner

cord was glued on, and the whole desk was given a base coat of white vinyl paint, then painted with coral enamel. This treatment made it an extremely attractive piece of furniture, quite functional, that goes well with its surroundings.

The next photo series shows the steps that were followed in reclaiming another discarded piece of furniture.

PHOTO SERIES 37
Redoing Furniture

1. The piece to be worked on is a cabinet, well constructed, but badly

scratched. A portion was cut out of the top to hold some type of machine—a record player, perhaps?

2. Our plan is not merely to refinish the cabinet, but to decorate it. Here

some schemes for applied ornamentation are tried out. Shapes of sun and moon, motifs used frequently in Spanish colo-

nial decor, have been cut from newspaper and pasted on the doors.

At the back of the top a band of scroll work with a central fan design (photo 7 of Series 7) is tried. It was decided that this band was overly ornate, so it was discarded.

3. The first step was to scrub all surfaces of the cabinet with soap and water.

Here rectangles of newspaper are glued on the end of the cabinet. The doors have been taken off. The screws that hold the hinges have been put in a plastic bag and tied to the cabinet so they won't be lost.

4. Beginning to fill the hole in the top. Rectangles of chipboard have been cut to

the proper size. Full strength glue is poured into the depression.

5. Putting rectangles of chipboard in place.

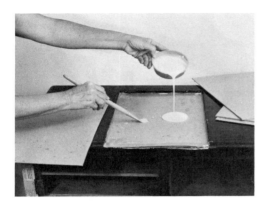

6. The depression has been filled. Mash was used at the front edge to continue the shape of the molding across the new portion that has been built up. Rectangles of newspaper are glued over the entire top.

7. Beginning to decorate one of the doors. Rectangles of newspaper have been glued in the central panel. Mash is patted in place on top of the newspaper. Circles and radial lines have been drawn for the outline of a sun face. Rays will be made from tubes of newspaper rolled on coat-hanger wire.

8. Modeling the sun face.

9. Completing the modeling of the sun face.

10. Corner ornaments like those shown in Step 2 will be used on the doors. Since there are eight corners it was decided to make a mold. Here plastilene is rolled.

11. It is shaped into the form of the ornament.

12. The ball of plastilene shown on the left has been cut in half. Here the curved ornament is carefully sliced in two.

13. Preparing to make the mold. The three pieces which form the corner ornament have been laid on a piece of plastic and pressed firmly into place. This is important—unless these small plastilene shapes are anchored securely they will float away when plaster is poured over them.

A retaining wall has been made of plastilene. This too must be firmly anchored and all corners must be squeezed together to prevent plaster from leaking out.

Mixing Plaster of Paris

Cold water is put into a container (in this case a plastic bowl). Plaster is sprinkled into the water until a mound of plaster projects above the surface of the water. The plaster is allowed to slake (soak up water) for a minute or two, then it is stirred with a long-handled spoon. The stirring is done from the bottom and the whole mass is agitated evenly. Plaster should be thoroughly mixed and air bubbles that form during the mixing should be broken, either with the spoon or by blowing on them. The plaster should be stirred until it just begins to thicken. When the spoon, in moving through the mixture, leaves a trace of its path, it is time to pour.

Pouring Plaster

14. The mixed plaster is poured over the model. The plaster must be poured

137

in a smooth stream without splashing. A small quantity should be poured on the model and then blown gently so that every portion of the model is covered with plaster. This must be done to avoid having air pockets in the mold. When all portions of the model have been covered with plaster, the pouring is continued until the space within the retaining wall is completely filled.

After the plaster has been poured the table should be rapped sharply with the fist so that any remaining air bubbles will be forced to the surface.

As plaster sets, the surface loses its shine and the mass starts to harden. In a few minutes it will be warm to the touch. After more time has elapsed, it will start to cool. When it is quite cold, the setting action is completed.

15. The mold has been turned over and the plastilene has been removed. A

spoon is used to refine the recesses in the mold.

It takes at least twenty-four hours for a mold to dry. It should not rest on a flat surface, but should be propped up so that air can circulate freely around it. Putting it in strong sunlight helps. (*Don't* put it in an oven.)

16. Pressing mash into the mold. The surface of the mold has been rubbed with vaseline and then wiped with a paper towel. Balls of mash have been rolled. Here mash is pressed into one of the recesses of the mold. (A popsicle stick is a good pressing tool.)

17. The mash has been pressed firmly into the mold. Excess moisture is blotted with a paper towel.

18. The pressed shapes have dried and have been removed from the mold. A bit of smoothing with sandpaper will be

needed before these are glued to the cabinet.

19. The decoration on the narrower door has been completed. The corner ornaments have been glued in place. The moon face and the corner ornaments have been brushed with gesso.

20. Heavy cord is used to form an ornament on the end of the cabinet. The surface has been given two coats of white vinyl paint. The ornament was drawn

on, here it is outlined in heavyweight cord. Pins are used to hold the cord in place while the glue sets.

21. Completing the cord ornament. Thinner cord was used for the smaller portions of the design. Mash was put into the center of the flower shape and given a crisscross pattern by pressing with a popsicle stick. Here diluted glue is brushed over the ornament.

22. Making the cord and mash ornament for the other end of the cabinet. This is a motif adapted from a gold headdress of a Mayan deity. A fork was used to score part of the design and a paring knife was used to "butter" (smooth) the rectangles of mash.

23. A layer of mash has been put on the top. A broom handle is used to roll the mash into a smooth surface. This completes the reconstruction of the cabinet. The cabinet was given a final coat of white vinyl; when this dried it was given a coat of white porcelain enamel. It was then antiqued to match the headboard (Photo Series 36). (See Color Plate 21.)

Chapter 15 · Making a Chair

THE next project is the making of a chair to be decorated in the same style as the pieces shown in Series 36, 37. The chair is made out of a salvaged fiber drum—a paper barrel used by manufacturers for shipping such things as dry chemicals.

PHOTO SERIES 38
Chair

1. Fiber drums have metal lids which fit into metal rings that are crimped to the top edge. Here a lid of a drum has been removed and the metal ring at the top has been cut off. The artist is cutting a portion out of the upper half of the drum.

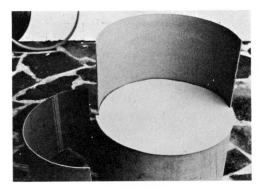

2. The portion cut out of the drum is shown at the lower left. A pattern of cardboard has been cut and fitted into the remaining portion of the drum. This pattern will be traced on a piece of plywood.

3. A piece of plywood has been cut to the shape of the pattern shown in Step 2. This will be the seat. A strip of wood 1 inch by 2 inches has been nailed on the underside of the plywood seat to keep it from warping. Additional strips of the same size have been nailed to the inner surface of the drum. These are placed at just the right height to support the seat when it is in position. The lower

141

ends of these wooden strips are attached to additional strips of the same measurement, which are nailed to the bottom of the drum. These strips (not visible in the picture) will receive casters in the last step of the construction.

4. A large sheet of chipboard is tried on the chair for size. The chipboard was cut so that it projected 1½ inches beyond the top and the ends of the back of the chair. These projecting portions

were cut to form tabs that could be folded around and glued to the fiberboard barrel. The sheet of chipboard was not long enough to wrap completely around the barrel, so an additional piece was cut to fill the space left at the front of the chair.

5. The chipboard has been glued to the drum, the tabs have been feathered, now they are being folded over the top of the back and glued in place. At the right of the picture, we see the tabs that have been folded around and glued to the end of the back.

6. The entire outer surface of the chair was covered with chipboard and

then with a layer of rectangular pieces of newspaper. The seat, which is removable, was covered, top and bottom, with newspaper and glue and the inside surface of the back of the chair was covered also.

7. Decorating. All surfaces of the chair were painted with two coats of white vinyl paint, followed by one coat of white porcelain enamel. A decorative

pattern of heavy and medium cord was glued to the surface. Corner ornaments of mash were pressed in the mold made in Photo Series 37 and attached at the top ends of the chair back.

When heavy cord is glued to fiber board and held in place by pins, there is a danger that, when the pins are pulled out, the cord will be pulled away with them. To prevent this, a fork is used to hold the cord in place while the pins are pulled out with a pair of pliers. After this, one coat of gold paint is brushed over the ornamentation.

8. Decorating the front portion of the chair. The design of cord has been completed. Here balls of mash are fastened

in place. Mash was put onto the surface of the chair with glue first, and then the ornaments were pressed into the mash. The excess mash is being removed with a brush.

9. Antiquing. Acrylic paint, raw umber and burnt sienna mixed in equal parts and thinned with water, is being brushed over a small portion of the surface. This is the same paint mixture that was used in the two preceding series.

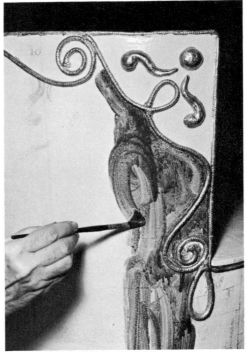

143

10. Wiping off the excess pigment.

11. A bit of cotton wrapped on a toothpick is used to wipe off some of the excess color from the small crevices of the design.

After the antiquing was completed, the ornament was given a final coat of gold paint.

When the decoration was completed, large ball-bearing casters were fastened to the bottom of the chair. Holes were bored through the base of the fiber drum and through the inner strips of wood

144

described in Step 3. The stems of the casters were inserted in these holes and were fastened with nuts and washers (Fig. 10).

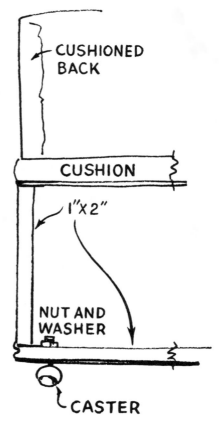

Fig. 10. Cross section of chair

Cushions for the chair. We suppose cushions *could* be made of papier mâché, but we doubt that they would be comfortable, so we turned to our local upholsterer for help. Using the cardboard pattern shown in Step 2, he made a 3-inch foam-rubber cushion for the seat and covered it with olive green crushed velvet. He took the portion that had been cut out of the drum (shown at lower left of picture 2), glued foam rubber to it and covered it with the same velvet, thus, making a curved cushion for the back of the chair. The finished chair with its casters and cushions in place is shown (Color Plate 19).

28. Clown with balloons and donkey

29. Large flower girl

30. Dancing girl
(back view),
holding balloons

31. Sunface

Chapter 16 · Light

IN Chapter 8 we saw that light may be an integral part of sculpture. In this chapter we shall explore some further ways of using light as an adjunct of paper constructions.

Candleholders can be made of cardboard. Cylindrical tubes for such candleholders can be made of fiberglass. When the fiberglass is decorated with patterns of torn tissue paper, the results are often extremely attractive.

PHOTO SERIES 39
Candle Lamps

1. The parts for making a candle-holder have been assembled, two circles, one 4½ inches in diameter, cut from corrugated cardboard, the other 5 inches in diameter, cut from chipboard; a strip of cardboard ½ inch wide, 13½ inches long; a strip of chipboard cut to the shape shown (the socket for the candle), three marbles for feet, and an iron washer for weight and stability.

2. Circles 4 inches in diameter are drawn on the two cardboard discs. Each of these circles is divided into six equal parts by using the radius of the circle to mark off equal distances on the circumference.

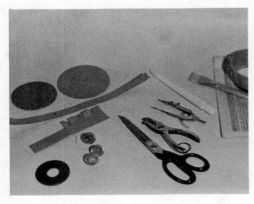
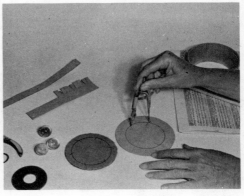

3. Six holes are punched in the larger disc; three are punched in the smaller disc.

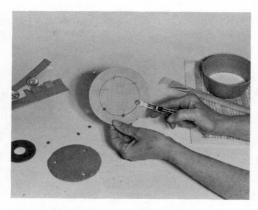

4. The socket for the candle is formed by wrapping the piece of chipboard around the base of the candle.

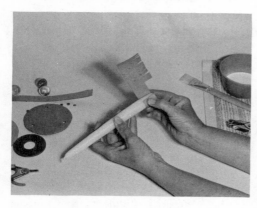

5. The strip forming the socket has been glued and is being held by a rubber band. The tabs have been folded up.

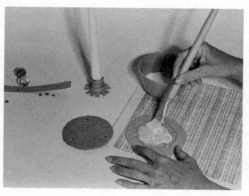

6. The two discs have been fastened together. Care was taken to see that the holes in the smaller disc coincided with the holes in the larger one. Glue is brushed onto the tabs of the candle socket.

7. The candle socket has been glued in place. The cardboard strip is being glued in place around the smaller disc. This will be the collar that holds the fiberglass cylinder.

8. The base has been turned over; the iron washer has been glued to the under-

side. Here the three marbles are being glued into position to serve as feet. Six holes were punched in the chipboard disc. Three of these holes coincide with holes punched in the smaller disc. The marbles are glued into the holes which do not coincide; thus three openings are left in the base for circulation of air.

9. Fiberglass comes in rolls 48 inches wide. Here a piece has been cut from the roll to form a cylinder 12 inches high. In order to wrap the collar of the candleholder, you must have a ½ inch overlap. The other dimension must be 13½ inches. Here the fiberglass is being tried in position. At the left is a small bottle of acrylic cement made especially for adhering fiberglass.

Note that the artist wears gloves while working with fiberglass to avoid getting painful splinters of glass in the skin.

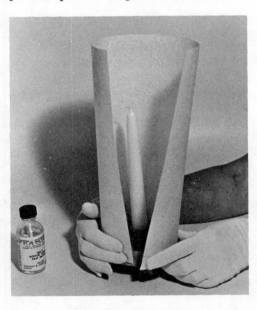

10. Brushing acrylic cement on the fiberglass. This cement must be put on both surfaces to be adhered; when the cement has dried the two surfaces are pressed together.

In a pinch white glue can be used instead of the acrylic cement. But the two surfaces of the fiberglass must be held

together until the glue sets. The acrylic cement is easier and quicker.

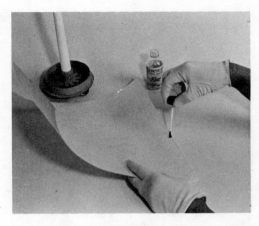

11. The finished cylinder in place on the candle holder.

Candle lampshades can be decorated in many ways. In Color Plate 24 we see three such shades. The one at the left—a montage of torn tissue paper, next to it an American flag design—also torn tissue paper, then a shade covered with a gift-wrap paper that shows old tobacco labels, and finally a shade on which color was sprayed against a stencil.

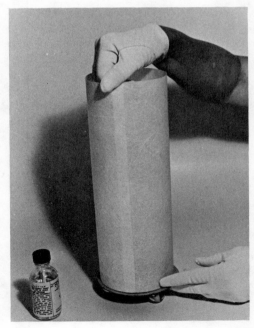

The next project shows an electric light fixture that uses a fiberglass cylinder similar to the one we made in the last series.

PHOTO SERIES 40
Light and Bracket

1. This shows a bracket that was made out of laminated strips of chipboard by the method demonstrated in Photo Series 18.

2. A fiberglass cylinder has been made as shown in Photo Series 39 and has been decorated with overlapping diamond shapes of pink and purple tissue paper. A circle of corrugated cardboard has been glued in one end of the cylinder. An electric light wire has been passed through the hole in the center of the cardboard circle. On the end of the wire inside the cylinder is a socket for a light bulb. A plug-in fixture will be added to the other end of the wire.

Here the artist is making a number of ornamental *S* shapes out of medium-weight cord by dipping pieces of the cord in glue, then laying them on a sheet of aluminum foil where they are held in position by pins.

3. The *S* shapes are linked together with short sections of thin wire.

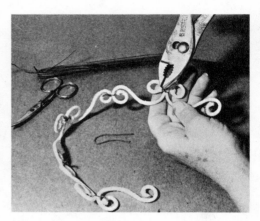

4. The *S* shapes linked together are glued to another cardboard circle the same size as the one fastened in the cylinder. This circle also has a hole in the center. When the ornamental band was put in place, the cardboard circle was slipped over the electric wire and glued to the circle in the top end of the cylinder.

Gold lacquer was brushed on the top. The bracket and the lamp are shown in use (Color Plate 22).

Another type of light fixture can be made by using a balloon and an ice-cream carton.

PHOTO SERIES 41
A Dome Light

1. A large balloon has been inflated and two iron washers have been tied to the valve. These will anchor the balloon in position in the ice-cream carton.

2. Paper toweling has been cut into wedge-shaped pieces. A layer of such pieces is being put over the balloon by laying the pieces on and patting them

with a wet sponge. No glue is used in this step. The purpose is to cover the visible portion of the balloon with wet paper towels. The pieces of toweling are wrinkled as they adhere to the balloon, but this wrinkling is just what we want.

3. Completing the layer of toweling.

4. After two layers of wet toweling had been applied to the balloon, three more layers of paper toweling were glued on. The toweling extended beyond the balloon and was glued to the carton. Here two lengths of mediumweight cord are glued to the dome shape just above the rim of the carton.

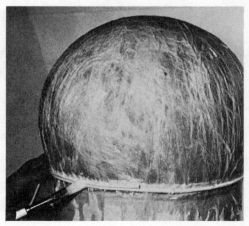

5. After the work was thoroughly dry a paring knife was used to cut through the dome at the level of the top rim of the carton. This, of course, punctured the balloon.

6. Despite our precautions, some of the glue seeped through the layers of wet toweling so that parts of the balloon stuck fast to the inside of the dome. A little work with a stiff nailbrush was needed to remove all traces of the balloon.

7. A lighting fixture to go with the dome has been constructed in the same manner that the candleholders were made in Photo Series 39. Two large circles of corrugated cardboard with holes punched in them were glued together so that the holes coincided. A collar to hold the dome was wrapped around and glued to the upper circle of cardboard. A wire with a socket at one end and a plug at the other is being fastened in place. Four marbles have been glued on the underside to serve as feet.

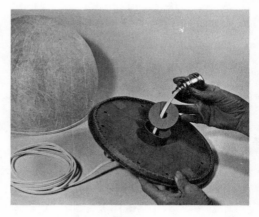

8. The dome light in use. The light passing through the wrinkled and overlapping layers of toweling produces a most interesting textural effect.

Color Plate 25 shows this dome light being held by the large flower girl seen in Chapter 8.

Another type of candleholder is a sconce, a decorative wall bracket which supports a dish that holds a candle socket. These are usually made of wrought iron, but by using the principles of lamination we can make one of chipboard.

PHOTO SERIES 42
Wall Sconce

1. A sketch has been made on a piece of newspaper; strips of chipboard ½ inch wide are being curled. When a strip of chipboard has been rolled into a tight circle and then released it will assume a graceful curve.

2. A pair of chipboard strips is placed on the sketch.

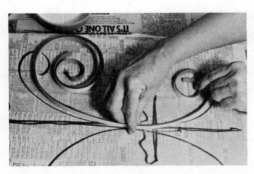

3. The strips are glued together.

4. After the strips have been glued together, they are covered with a layer of newspaper and glue. The newspaper is torn into 1-inch-wide strips about 8 inches long (across the page). These strips are glued to the side of the laminated chipboard design. The portion that projects above the chipboard is torn into tabs which are folded over and glued. Since the newspaper strips were torn across the page, the tearing of the tabs is with the grain of the paper.

Covering the chipboard strips with the newspaper strengthens the lamination.

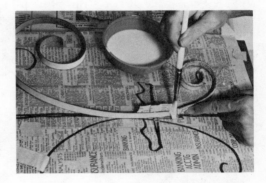

5. Two ½-inch strips of mounting board are added to the lamination, one on the inside and one on the outside.

The end of the shape has been formed into a modified leaf design.

6. Four strips of chipboard will form the upright central portion of the sconce. Here a bracket cut from two pieces of chipboard stapled together is being fastened into the upright stem. A loop of chipboard fastened at the end of the bracket will support the candle dish.

7. A spiral made of two strips of chipboard laminated together is attached to the upper end of the stem.

8. Stapling the outer rim of the candle dish. At the left is a chipboard circle and a chipboard ring. These will be fastened in place as shown in Fig. 11. In the upper center is the candle socket.

Fig. 11. Sconce

9. The sconce hangs on a wall while the portions of the construction are as-

152

sembled. The two side pieces have been tied temporarily to the central stem.

10. A shade of fiberglass is tried on the sconce. It was decided later that the design was better without the shade, so it was discarded.

11. Making a floral design at the top of the sconce. Heavy cord is being formed into loops suggesting flower petals and is being glued in place. Before this was done, a collar was made of three pieces of chipboard stapled together. An opening was made in the collar so that the stem and its circle at the top could

be placed in the collar. This was done so that the flower petals would be attached, not at the back of the circle, but in the midportion of the rim. The chipboard collar covered with a sheet of plastic, the sconce was put in place and the petal loops were shaped, glued, and fastened to the collar with pins while the glue set. Circles drawn on the collar served as guidelines in placing the cord loops.

Small balls of mash (seen in the foreground) were glued at the base portions of the petal designs and pressed into place with the handle of a paintbrush.

12. Mediumweight cord was wound around the central stem, an additional loop of chipboard was added at the bottom of the stem. The sconce was given two base coats of white vinyl paint.

The next step was to scumble a coral acrylic paint over the floral portion and a light green acrylic over the central stem and leaves. When these dried, the sconce was given a coat of gold lacquer (Color Plate 23).

Here is still another combination of light with paper construction.

PHOTO SERIES 43
A Bird in a Gilded Cage

1. We are going to make use of a shape like the fluted cone that was developed in photo 7 of Series 7. A circle with an 18-inch diameter has been cut out of chipboard. Radial lines have been drawn dividing the circle into twenty-four equal sectors.

Cuts 1½ inches long are made from the center on every other radial line.

2. The circle is folded backward and forward on the radial lines. The square edge of the worktable helps in this step.

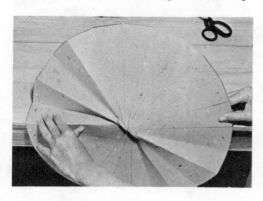

3. Another circle with an 18-inch diameter has been drawn and cut out. One quarter of the circle was removed (see Fig. 12) and the remainder was rolled into a cone.

154

This will be the inner portion of the top of the birdcage. The base of the cone has a diameter of 13½ inches. Twelve holes, the same distance apart, are punched near the rim of the cone. Cuts have been made at the top portion of the cone similar to those made in Step 1.

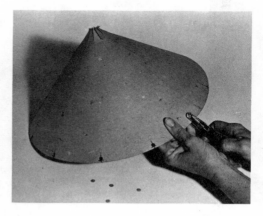

4. A lining of aluminum foil is glued to the inner surface of the cone. The lining is so placed that it does not cover the holes.

5. A light cord with a socket attached has been threaded through a cylinder, a section cut from the core of a roll of paper toweling, then through the opening in the apex of the cone, and finally

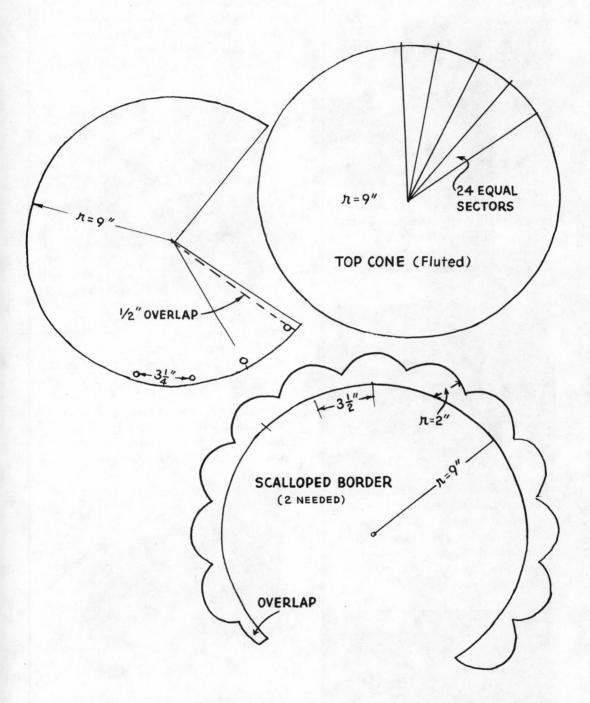

r = 9″

½″ OVERLAP

3¼″

24 EQUAL
SECTORS

r = 9″

TOP CONE (Fluted)

3½″

r = 2″

SCALLOPED BORDER
(2 NEEDED)

r = 9″

OVERLAP

Fig. 12. Bird cage

through a hole pierced in a styrofoam ball.

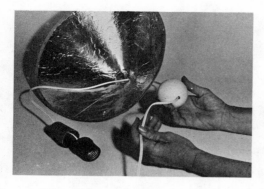

6. The light socket and the cylinder have been glued in place. Here a trapeze for the bird is being made out of a tube of newspaper rolled on coat-hanger wire with a piece of string threaded through it.

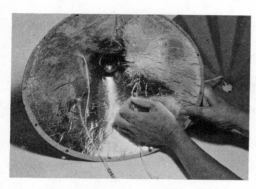

7. The fluted cone we made (Steps 1, 2) is attached to the inner cone so that the angles between the flutings come midway between the holes punched in the inner cone. Glue was brushed on the angles, and pins hold the construction together while the glue sets.

8. Attaching the top portion of the fluted cone to the cylinder that holds the light socket with strips of paper and glue. The styrofoam ball has been glued in place at the top of the cylinder and the joint has been covered with paper and glue.

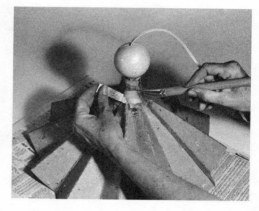

9. Making the floor of the cage: a circle 13½ inches in diameter was cut from corrugated cardboard. Twelve holes were punched equal distances apart, ½ inch in from the edge. Here a strip of chipboard ½ inch wide is wrapped around the circumference of the circle and glued into place to form a flange. Flange in place, all surfaces of the floor were covered with paper and glue.

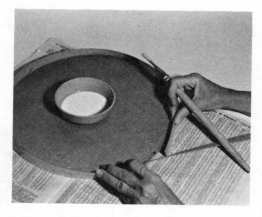

10. Beginning to assemble the parts of the cage. The top rests upside down in a cylindrical waste basket. Twelve tubes have been made of newspaper rolled

around a coat-hanger wire. These will be the bars of the cage (coat-hanger wire removed, of course). The bars will be slipped through the holes in the inner cone and the ends will be glued inside the flutings of the top (full-strength glue used here). All of the bars are the same length.

In the right rear is another circle 13½ inches in diameter cut from corrugated cardboard with twelve holes ½ inch in from the edge, the same distance apart. This will be a temporary guide in assembling the parts of the cage. In the lower right corner are two pieces of corrugated cardboard notched so that they will fit into each other, forming a cross. The pieces of cardboard are 5 inches wide and 15 inches long. Pieces ½ inch wide and 13½ inches long have been cut out of each side of the two pieces of cardboard.

11. The parts of the cage assembled: the two pieces of cardboard (described in Step 10) have been put together, the resultant cross rests on the inner cone of the top of the cage. The temporary circle rests on top of the cardboard cross. The bars of the cage have been placed so that they pass through the temporary cardboard circle. The floor of the cage is in position with the ends of the bars projecting through the holes that were punched in it. Note that the flange projects downward from the floor (upward in this picture). When the parts were

assembled, strips of damp newspaper were glued to the ends of the bars (full-strength glue) which project through the floor of the cage. When this operation was completed the cage was allowed to remain resting in the basket overnight to permit the glue to harden. When the construction was dry, the temporary circle was cut away from the bars and removed, the two pieces of cardboard forming the cross brace were slipped apart and removed also.

The final step in the construction of the cage was attaching the two scalloped bands shown in the diagram (Fig. 12).

12. A bird for the cage. After what we have learned about making patterns it should be simple to make a bird to swing on the perch in the cage. At the left of this picture are three shapes cut from a piece of mounting board (this mounting board has one brown side and one white). The artist is rolling a cone of kraft paper which will be the head and the beak. Note the coin resting on the portion that will be the bird's tail—

157

this is a weight to balance the bird on his perch.

13. Assembling the bird. The piece seen in the upper left-hand corner of the previous picture was turned over and stapled to the large piece in such a way that it will bulge outward to form a chest.

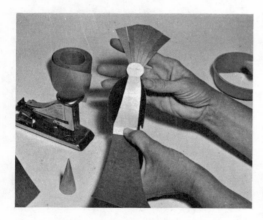

14. Continuing the assembling. The sides of the pattern of the bird have been

folded up and strips of package tape have been pasted across the sides and the chest. Glue has been brushed on the two tail strips, and these will be laminated together in a curve. At the left of the picture is the cone that was rolled for the head and beak. Tabs have been cut and folded inward.

15. The two portions forming the tail have been glued and stapled together with the coin between them. Glue is being brushed on the tabs of the beak.

16. The construction of the bird is completed. He balances happily on the artist's finger.

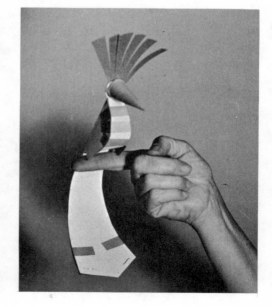

17. The bird swings on his perch in the cage while the light above his head shines on his crest.

All parts of the bird and the cage were given a basic coat of white vinyl paint. A decoration of mediumweight cord was glued to the scalloped borders at the top and bottom of the cage, then the cage was given two coats of gold lacquer.

The bird was painted with fluorescent and nonfluorescent acrylics. Pieces of gift-wrap paper were cut into feather shapes and glued to the tail. The bird was then given several coats of clear lacquer, sprayed on.

The finished cage and bird are shown hanging on an outdoor terrace (Color Plate 26).

Chapter 17 · Fantasy

WE have already made one dragon, why make another? Well, for two reasons—first, we received a commission to make a larger dragon and we did so. The dragon was put on display in a toy store. Secondly, going through the steps of making a large dragon will give us an opportunity to review the processes of papier mâché construction. (And besides—making dragons is fun!)

PHOTO SERIES 44
Large Dragon

1. A balloon was covered with mash. When the mash dried, full-strength glue was brushed on.

2. Starting to make a neck. A strip of chipboard was cut and stapled, as shown in Fig. 13, to make a sectional tube with

tabs. A long, thin balloon was slipped inside the tube and inflated.

3. Pieces of chipboard are fastened between the tabs with strips of kraft paper and glue. This makes the curve in the neck permanent.

4. A long, tapering strip of chipboard has been wound around a piece of garden hose to form a dragon tail. The chipboard was rolled into a tight cylinder first—this made it easier to wind into a serpentine form. One end of the garden hose has been tied to the leg of a chair for temporary support.

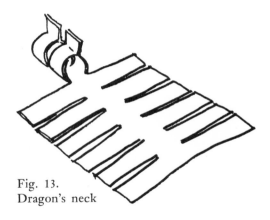

Fig. 13.
Dragon's neck

5. Papering the tail.

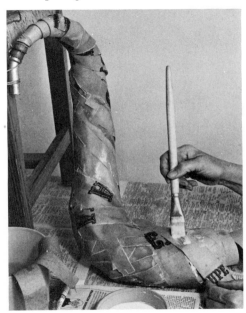

6. Attaching a leg.

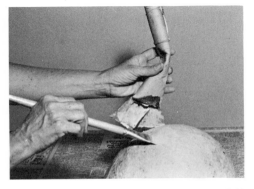

7. Attaching the second leg.

8. Neck, tail, and body have been assembled. A box (the same one we used for the owl in Series 5) is tried as a head.

9. A different head has been roughly shaped. One arm has been attached.

10. Making claws: strips of chipboard are filled with mash and pressed into place on the hand.

11. Covering the dragon with mash: two arms have been attached. Here mash is put on the tail and squeezed into shape.

12. A curlicue for the end of the tail is made from a short piece of rope.

13. The piece of rope, covered with mash, must be supported while it dries.

15. A block of wood helps in modeling surface planes.

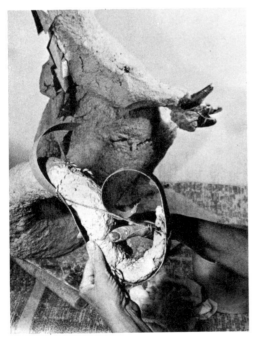

14. The claws on the feet were made the same way as those on the hands. Here feet and legs are being covered with mash.

16. More modeling with the wooden block.

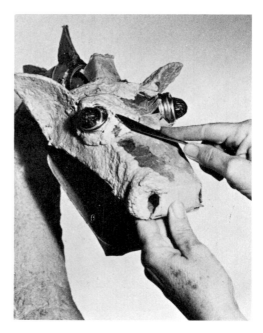

17. Papering the head. A section of mailing tube has been put in the mouth as a temporary bit. A rubber band holds the jaws in position.

19. The head nearly completed. Dentures have been made for the lower jaw; eyebrows have been shaped; the nostrils have been given flaring edges. The tabs on the neck have been cut into triangular spines and covered with mash.

18. The head has been fastened to the neck, ears have been attached, and holes have been made for the nostrils. Two bicycle reflector buttons, fastened to two metal tops from 35 mm film tubes, serve as eyes.

Mash is applied to the head and modeled to form facial features.

164

20. Oops! We almost forgot horns.

21. The dragon has been completed—all but the tongue. Horns are in place, fangs have been put in the upper jaw and spines like those in Series 21 have been attached to the tail. Two coats of white vinyl paint have been brushed over the entire figure. The dragon was then given coats of acrylic and fluorescent paints. The tongue was made the same way as the tongue in Series 21—it was painted, coated with a clear lacquer and then glued into place. When all was secure and dry, the horns, spines, and claws were given two coats of gold lacquer and then the dragon was given two coats of clear spray-on lacquer.

Dragons are good subjects for papier mâché sculpture because they allow complete freedom to the artist in deciding on proportions and modeling anatomical details. (No one can tell you that the nose isn't right or that the arms are too long.)

As we mentioned earlier, our dragon was used as a display in a toy store.

While we are on the subject of toys, let's make a figure whose head, neck and legs can move. We'll do this by modeling all the parts of plastilene separately, covering them with shells of paper and glue, cutting the shells and removing the plastilene (as we did in Series 21), then putting the shells back together and assembling them with rubber bands.

PHOTO SERIES 45
A Jointed Donkey

1. Plastilene has been rolled into a cylinder and cut into four pieces. These will be legs.

2. Tapering the legs. The piece at the left will be the body.

3. Cutting a head.

4. The body has been shaped and placed on a wooden prop that is fastened to the center of a turntable. Sockets to receive the legs and the neck have been cut in the body with a spoon.

The neck has been rolled and a socket has been made in the head to receive it.

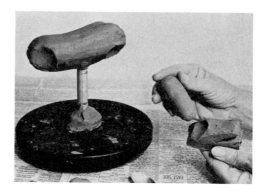

5. Trying the parts together. A mouth has been cut in the head. Head and neck are held in place by toothpicks. A tail is tried for size.

6. Papering the end of a leg.

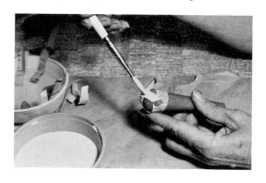

7. Completing the papering of the leg by rolling and gluing damp newspaper around it. Care is taken not to glue the paper to the plastilene.

8. Papering the body. Four layers of dampened paper will be glued on—first newspaper, then kraft paper, then newspaper again, and a final layer of kraft paper.

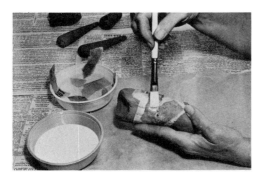

9. The work has dried overnight. The artist cuts a section out of the back with a razor blade.

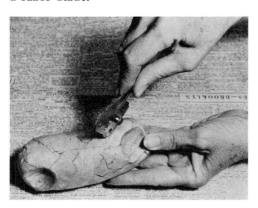

10. The plastilene is removed from the body. Note that the section cut out does not include any of the sockets.

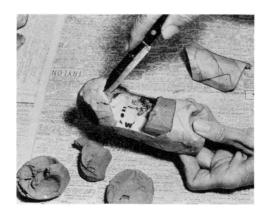

11. A leg has been cut into two parts. The plastilene is being removed.

12. Before the two parts of the leg are sealed back together, one end of a rubber band must be fastened inside. A short

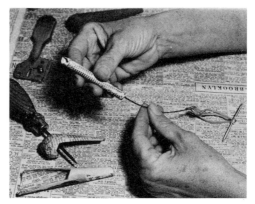

167

tube of newspaper has been rolled and a rubber band with a toothpick attached to the other end is being threaded through it. (The purpose of the tube is to give extra tension to the rubber band.)

A hole has been pierced in the upper end of the leg with an ice pick.

13. The rubber band is threaded through the hole in the top of the leg. After this is done, the ends of the toothpick will be cut off (leaving enough to anchor the rubber band in place) and the two parts of the leg will be sealed together with paper and glue. A bit of wire is left in the free end of the rubber band to keep it from slipping back into the leg and being lost.

16. A pair of ears cut from chipboard are attached to a piece of fine milliner's wire passing through the head. (Any very thin wire would do.)

14. The head cut into two parts.

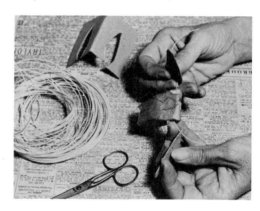

17. Pieces of newspaper have been glued on the ears to cover the wire. Excess paper is trimmed off.

15. Digging the plastilene out of the head with a hairpin.

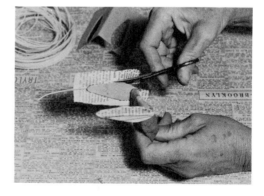

18. The two parts of the head are sealed together with one end of a rubber band fastened inside.

168

19. The rubber band from the head has been threaded through the neck and into the body. A piece of milliner's wire has been passed through the rubber band; this will be pulled through the rear of the body and fastened. This wire will become part of the tail.

20. The rest of the rubber bands are fastened together inside the body by means of milliner's wire. The band from the left front leg is attached to the band from the right rear leg; the band from the right front is attached to the left rear.

21. The section cut out of the back is put in place. The joint will be sealed with paper and glue.

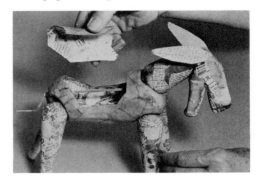

22. A piece of mediumweight cord is tied with thread to the wire at the back end to form the tail. The place where the tail touches the body will be covered with paper and glue. When attached, the tail will be trimmed to the right length and the end frayed slightly.

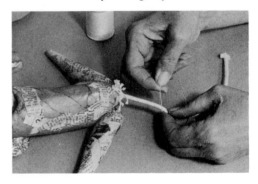

23. The completed donkey. His mane is cord and it is painted black.

24. The donkey and a friend—a clown with movable limbs, who was made the same way as the donkey. This pair is shown again in Color Plate 28.

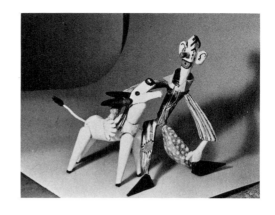

Chapter 18 · Sculpture for the Garden

THE duck whose construction we saw in photos 8, 9, and 10 of Series 14 proved to be a fun addition to our garden, and so did "Long leg" (photos 11 and 12 of the same series). We liked them so much that we made a few more, some of them using balloons and others using patterns. Here are the steps we used in making a pair of our Yard Birds:

PHOTO SERIES 46
Yard Bird 1

1. This bird is made from pieces of chipboard cut according to the pattern

shown in Fig. 14. (Note: you don't need to copy this pattern—you can use it as a point of departure in creating your own. If you do use the pattern, you need not follow it slavishly because, if you make the bird fatter, or thinner, or longer or shorter, what does it matter?)

2. Fastening the shape with staples.

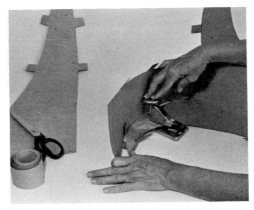

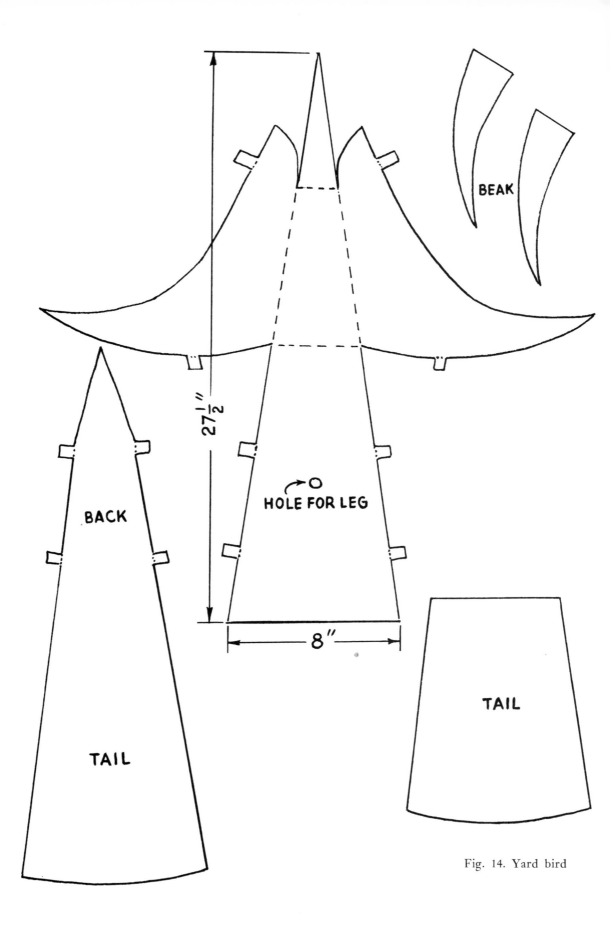

BEAK

BACK

TAIL

HOLE FOR LEG

$27\frac{1}{2}''$

$8''$

TAIL

TAIL

Fig. 14. Yard bird

3. Sealing the joints with gummed paper (package tape).

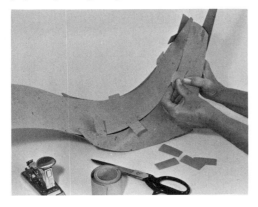

4. The two pieces that form the beak are stapled together along the top edge. A piece of coat-hanger wire has been shaped to form a crest.

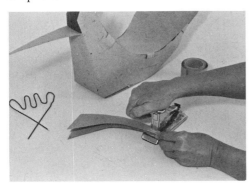

5. The crest and the beak are tried in place. When the position is right, a stapler is used to fasten the beak to the head.

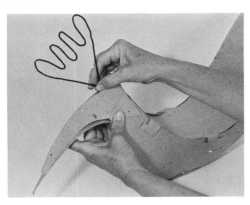

6. The beak and the crest have been fastened in place. Joints have been sealed with kraft paper and glue.

The second piece, which forms the tail, has been attached to the end of the body. The two tail pieces are formed into a curve. They will be stapled together in this position so that the tail will hold the curve (lamination).

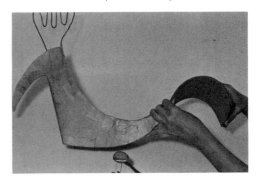

7. A piece of ½-inch wooden dowel, 24 inches long, is used for a leg. Here the dowel is held erect by being stuck into the end of a carton, while a nail is driven into the back of the bird to hold the dowel in position.

The other end of the dowel (the part that goes into the ground) has been sharpened in a pencil sharpener. Two bricks inside the carton make it a support for the bird during the remainder of the construction.

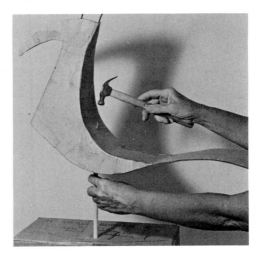

8. Preparing to apply mash. Spoonfuls of mash are patted into a pancake shape on a piece of newspaper.

9. Rolling the mash into a layer. A second sheet of newspaper has been put on top of the pancake and the mash is rolled between the two sheets.

10. The top sheet of newspaper is pulled away.

11. The bottom sheet with the layer of mash is lifted, turned over and laid on the bird (where glue was brushed first) and pressed firmly into place. The newspaper is then peeled away.

12. A paring knife is used to press the surface smooth. This process is continued until every portion of the bird has been covered with mash.

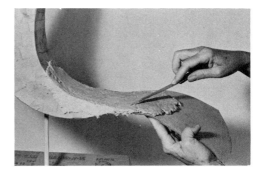

13. The metal cover from a 35mm film box is pressed into the head to serve as an eye.

This completes the construction of the bird—he must now be set aside to dry.

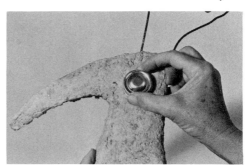

14. The finished bird. He was given two coats of silicone followed by two coats of white vinyl paint, then some areas were painted with fluorescent paint and other areas with nonfluorescent paint. When the colors were dry, the bird was given two coats of marine varnish. He is seen again in Color Plate 27.

PHOTO SERIES 47
Yard Bird 2

Another yard bird made over a balloon.

1. A strip of chipboard has been cut as shown. The projecting portion will form the tail of our bird.

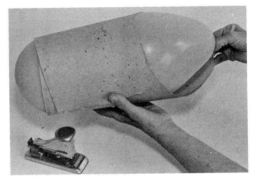

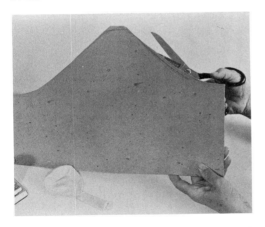

3. Another piece of chipboard for the underside of the tail is fastened in place with a strip of gummed paper.

2. The chipboard has been rolled and stapled to form a tube. A balloon has been inflated inside the tube.

4. All exposed portions of the balloon are covered with strips of kraft paper and glue.

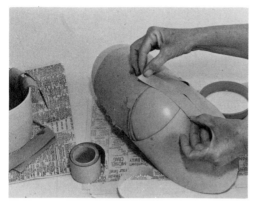

5. A beak made of two pieces of chipboard has been fastened in place and covered with paper and glue. Here a layer of mash is applied.

6. The layer of mash is smoothed.

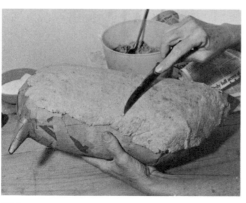

7. Two legs have been fastened in the body by the method shown in Series 46. The bird is given two coats of silicone and a basic coat of white vinyl paint.

8. The finished bird—painted with fluorescent and nonfluorescent colors.

9. Another bird of the same family—made in the same way. These two birds are shown in Color Plate 27.

These yard birds are free to move about. The silicone and varnish have made them weather resistant. Their forms are streamlined, and this is most important in any piece of papier mâché sculpture that is to be placed outdoors. Any fold in the surface that will catch and hold water will prove fatal.

Another piece of garden sculpture is the dancing girl who is seen balancing on one toe in Color Plate 30. This figure was made the same way as the mermaid described in Series 35 with one important difference—the figure had to be planned so that she could stand on one toe.

To make this possible we needed a steel rod embedded in a heavy block of cement. A local manufacturer of cement pipe, tile and the like made such a construction for us. Here are the steps in building the figure.

PHOTO SERIES 48
Dancing Girl

1. The form is planned on a small armature like the one shown (Plate 8).

2. A cardboard tube has been rolled and slipped over the metal rod that is embedded in the cement block. Another longer tube of chipboard has been rolled. This tube will be slipped over the first one and the space between the two tubes will be filled with strips of paper and glue.

3. Beginning the construction of a skeleton. A tube for the second leg has been attached and tubes for arms are temporarily in place.

4. Chipboard has been cut and folded to form the upper portion of the torso. This has been attached to another tube which will be the neck.

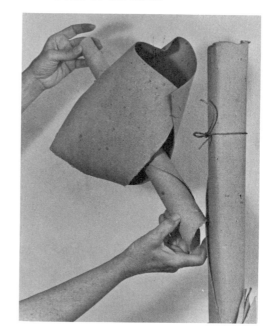

5. The arms have been put back in position.

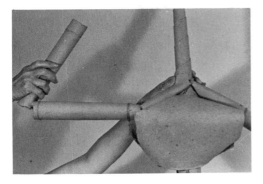

6. An elbow joint is bent and reinforced. Pieces of twine are used to hold the arms in position.

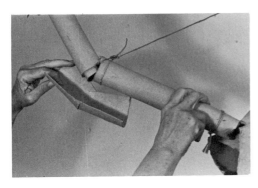

7. A strip of chipboard to form the waist.

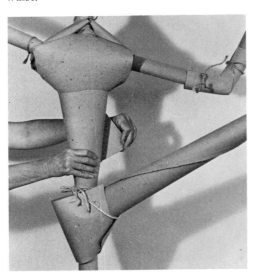

8. Preparing to make the head by putting a layer of mash on a balloon. Mash is rolled on a sheet of newspaper.

9. This is wrapped around a balloon.

10. The balloon covered with mash is hung up to dry.

11. The head has dried and been put in position on the neck. Portions of the figure have been covered with newspaper and glue. Here a strip of chipboard has been used to build up the shape of a thigh. After this the completed figure was covered with newspaper and glue. The hands were formed in the same manner as those of the mermaid in Series 35. The rest of the figure was covered with mash and anatomical details were modeled before the mash dried.

12. The figure has been given two coats of silicone and two coats of white vinyl paint. A hole was made in the big toe of her left foot to hold a bird like the one made in Series 8. Another bird made like the one in Series 43 balances on her right hand. After this, a wig with a Psyche knot was made of paper and mash. No color was put on the figure except for a circlet of flowers made of bread paste that was wrapped around her Psyche knot.

Anatomical details were modeled in extremely simplified form.

The cement block holding the rod that supports this figure was concealed among the stones in a rock garden so that when the figure is in place on the rod, she gives the illusion of dancing on air. The figure can be turned in any direction. She is so light that she can be easily picked up and carried indoors.

Another piece of garden sculpture is the large flower girl we saw holding the light in Color Plate 29. In that picture she was indoors. Color Plate 29 shows her beside a pool holding a bouquet.

180

PHOTO SERIES 49
Sun Face

A final garden sculpture—a sun face:

1. A circle 30 inches in diameter has been cut out of a piece of plywood, part of a packing case. By means of a string, a nail, and a felt marker, a concentric circle is drawn, this will serve as a guide in attaching strips of wood to hold the sun's rays.

2. Strips of wood for the rays have been nailed on. (Odds and ends of wood strips.)

3. Making a dome shape: a circle of chipboard was cut out. Cuts were made

along radial lines from the outer edge halfway into the center. The sectors were overlapped and stapled. This made a dome.

4. A cylinder of chipboard with tabs cut at the top and bottom will serve as a support for the center of the dome.

5. The chipboard dome has been fastened in place with glue and nails.

6. Strips of newspaper are glued over the chipboard dome.

181

7. A layer of mash is rolled onto the dome.

8. The layer of mash is shaped with a wooden block.

After this step the work was allowed to dry so that the shell of mash would be strong enough to support further modeling.

9. A drawing of a sun face has been made on a circle of newspaper with a felt marking pen. (Note: Some felt markers are "permanent"; the lines made by these will not bleed when they are

182

wet. In this case a nonpermanent type was used.)

10. The drawing has been laid face down upon the mash dome. A wet sponge is patted on the newspaper. This transfers the lines of the drawing to the mash. (It also makes the lines of the drawing show through the newspaper.)

11. The drawing shows on the mash.

12. More mash has been applied and features are being modeled.

13. The wooden strips were brushed with glue and the rays are modeled with mash squeezed onto the projecting strips.

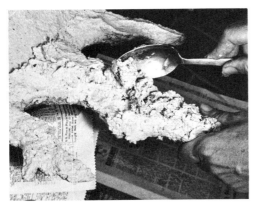

14. A paper towel is used to blot excess water from the rays, after this the rays were modeled with a spoon.

15. Further modeling of the features.

16. Modeling has been completed, the work was allowed to dry, then front and back were given two coats of silicone, followed by two coats of white vinyl paint. The work was allowed to stand (upside down) in full sunlight to hasten final drying. After this the front of the sculpture was given one coat of bright red lacquer, then two coats of antique gold lacquer were scumbled on in such manner that portions of red lacquer showed through. Finally, both front and back were given two coats of marine varnish. Color Plate 31 shows this sun face hanging on a vine covered wall.

Chapter 19 · L'envoi

THE art of papier mâché is one of the oldest—and one of the youngest. The Chinese invented it about two thousand years ago, yet as a recognized art form it is in its infancy. It is only within recent years that it has been accepted as a worthy material for the talents of the creative artist. Forms designed with feeling, imagination, and originality have merit, be they made of clay, metal, stone, wood, or paper.

One of the reasons for the resurgence of interest in papier mâché as an art form has been the amazing number of technical developments—the new pigments available to the artist, the new adhesives, the great improvements and variety in paper itself.

So many new products have become available to the artist that one is apt to be bewildered. What to choose?

In our work we felt duty bound to try everything that we could lay our hands upon, all the varieties of paste and glues and lacquers and varnishes and polymer mediums and acrylics, etc., etc. You, too, will want to experiment. Certainly you will want to keep abreast of latest developments for, even as we go to press, new pigments, new adhesives may be coming from the industrial laboratories. After you have tried everything, you will do as we have done and simplify the assortment of materials you use.

For example, paste and glue. There are many individual preferences among the artists who work in papier mâché. Some set great store by wheat paste (wallpaper paste). This is inexpensive, easy to prepare, and makes good adhesive for most paper work. It has one serious drawback—it spoils quickly, so small quantities should be mixed at a time.

Some artists like to make their own paste out of flour by mixing flour with a little water, then slowly adding more water to bring it to a thin milky consistency, then heating with constant stirring until the paste thickens and becomes creamy.

184

We have found making our own paste a waste of time. We found another drawback, too—bugs sometimes like the taste of the finished products made with flour paste.

Among other adhesives used for special jobs are starch and rubber cement.

The polymer mediums (acrylic polymer emulsions) are used as mediums for mixing and glazing acrylic colors. They also serve as adhesives and primers. They come in mat and gloss finishes.

We have come to rely almost entirely upon the white synthetic glue, acrylic colors and the polymer media.

Another word about priming or sizing. All work in paper should have an undercoating of some kind before it is painted and decorated. White glue is good, the polymer mediums or any exterior paint thinned with turpentine or with water if it is a water-base paint. As you can see from the step-by-step series described in earlier chapters, our favorite primer is a base coat of white exterior vinyl paint. For anything intended for use outdoors, we prime with liquid silicone and then brush exterior paint over it.

For final treatment of surfaces, the artist in papier mâché may choose from various lacquers, enamels, polymer mediums and any one of the many spray-on finishes. We do most of our work with acrylic paints and spray-on lacquers.

While we are on the subject of finished surfaces we should say a word about Spackle. This is patching plaster. Small quantities mixed with water will form a smooth creamy paste, which can be brushed over surfaces to achieve an ivory, smooth finish. Any streaks left by the brush may be smoothed with fine sandpaper after the work is dried. A little white glue added to Spackle makes an excellent gesso.

In the preceding chapters we have tried to suggest the simplest way of working and the simplest materials to use. Another example of the simplification of our palette is the use of gold paint. We no longer struggle with gold leaf for we find the ready-mixed or prepared gold paint is easier to use and just as satisfactory. When we want a deeper, richer tone of gold, we add a bit of bronze powder.

As one works with papier mâché, one discovers new uses for the material. We almost forgot to mention its value for repair jobs. When we installed the bracket and light shown in Photo Series 40, we made a small but ugly hole in the wall—too small to warrant mixing up a batch of plaster. Paper mash proved to be just right to fill up the hole.

It came in handy for another repair job. On our outdoor terrace we have a pair of metal wall lamps. We knew, of course, that these should be painted from time to time, but—well, you know how it is—the spirit of mañana and all that! One day the lower portion of one of the lamps rusted through and fell off. We could not find another lamp to match, so we tried sealing the lower portion back on with paper and glue, fabricating a missing ball pendant out of mash. It worked. (Incidently, on this same outdoor terrace hang the two plaques shown in Plate 13. These have weathered sun and rain for several years, and it looks as if they will outlast our metal lamps, even if we do remember to paint the lamps again when they need it.)

There have been other repair jobs as well—replacing an ornament broken from an old Spanish Colonial cabinet, replacing a missing piece from a chess set, and repairing portions of a rococo picture frame.

We have tried to share all that we have found out about papier mâché but there is still much more to learn. Work in this medium will be not only creation, but will also be exploration. One must be daring to try the new and the unusual.

One of the most valuable tools of the artist is his sketch book—keep one handy and jot down ideas as they come to you. Do three-dimensional sketching also, with cardboard, scissors and stapler. This is lots of fun and it leads often to original aesthetic forms.

Is papier mâché a hobby? Yes, it is—one of the best—but it is more. It can lead to a career.

In the course of our research on paper we learned that the United States today uses more than half of all the paper produced in the entire world— over four hundred pounds per year for each man, woman and child. What eventually becomes of all this paper? A small portion achieves immortality in libraries and in art collections. Some paper is used in buildings as insulation, but most of it ends up in rubbish fires, scattering soot on the landscape and fouling the air we breathe. What a shame! How much better if we could find worthwhile uses for the paper for which we have sacrificed our trees— and add beauty, instead of ugliness, to our world.

Well, it is time to say goodbye—we hope you have as much fun working with our book as we had in writing it.

Index

Photo: C. W. Cadarette

About the Authors

JOHN B. KENNY is well known to artists everywhere for his three books, *The Complete Book of Pottery Making, Ceramic Sculpture* and *Ceramic Design.*

The enormous success of these books, their adoption by a large number of schools, colleges and universities, as well as by artists and craftsmen, is due to the author's wide background as a skilled potter and experienced teacher. For over twenty years Mr. Kenny was principal of the High School of Art and Design, New York City's specialized high school for preparing young people for professional careers as artists and designers.

Examples of Mr. Kenny's work are included in private collections in this country and in Europe. He holds the degree of Master of Fine Arts in ceramics from Alfred University and is a member of the Society of Illustrators.

CARLA KENNY, an illustrator of note in her own right and also a member of the Society of Illustrators, did illustrations for John Kenny's *Ceramic Design.* This is her second collaboration in writing a book with Mr. Kenny. The first was *The Art of Papier Mâché.*

John and Carla Kenny and their daughter, Pamela, live in Cuernavaca, Mexico.